I0621234

Good to Greatness

Published by
Hybrid Global Publishing
333 E 14th Street
#3C
New York, NY 10003

Monaghan, Christine.
Good To Greatness
    ISBN: 978-1-957013-77-0
    eBook: 978-1-957013-78-7
    LCCN: 2023905378

Cover design by: Natasha Clawson
Cover photo by: Jeremy Bishop
Copyediting by: Claudia Volkman
Interior design by: Suba Murugan

www.christinemonaghan.com/reset

Dedication

Most of us are completely unprepared for grief's wrath. We need to do a much better job of standing next to those navigating grief in all forms—the invisible twists and turns linger long after loss itself. We need to give ourselves the grace of time. Grief demonstrates the depth of love, passion, and connection to the human being or object that's no longer in original form. Loss shows up as a dear one passing away; an Olympic dream ended before full ascension; a relationship of mutual love no longer serving each other; a disease altering one's life; a business vision that crumbles. No one is exempt from grief. The sought-after outcome? The choice to focus forward, utilize loss to create greatness for oneself and others; replace anger, sadness, and bitterness with love, compassion, and grace; build strengths not recognized prior; and to have reverence for still having the privilege to live, today.

My mum and dad both left Planet Earth within a month of each other—Mum on December 22, 2021, and Dad on January 29, 2022. Mum's demise was expected, yet no less painful. Dad? Completely unexpected despite being ninety-three. He was living independently, still driving, and 100 percent cognitively on point. Why couldn't he have waited . . . just a bit? We, his grown adult kids, needed him, but it wasn't to be. Our choice? Become one another's anchor despite our collective resistance to this harsh, inconvenient reality. A year later, it feels like we left both parents behind in 2022.

Untangling grief is confusingly complicated. Embracing the gift in loss is essential—acknowledging the privilege of another lovely day on planet earth to hear birds sing, to give and receive greatness. The privileges of being the daughter of Bob and Kath are: my existence as a result of theirs (everything!); their presence within me, in the best ways possible; their ingrained voice championing me forward ("way to go, keep punchin!"). Their mottos to the four siblings: "Be a leader, not a follower" (Mum) and "What's more fun than fun?" (Dad).

Mum and Dad, the gift of your loss is carrying forward the greatness you provided; not one day passed that I didn't feel adored; you championed my outlandish interests; blessed me with the gift of humor and fun; instilled confidence in me socially and expression of my voice; demonstrated humility in your remarkable experiences; and showed perseverance and resilience through life's inevitable struggles and losses. To all my lovely days of greatness ahead in simplest form. You're both immensely loved and appreciated, daily.

Contents

Contents

Introduction

Liberation // *liberate somebody/something (from somebody/something);
to free a country or a person from the control of someone/something else.*

Moving from *good to greatness* in one's life is about liberation of self
and circumstances that are not serving us. We all seek liberation for
our lives—packaged differently, yet the common intention is to be and
create freedom as individually defined. This book focuses on moving
from good to greatness in the following areas:

- Financial freedom
- Economic innovation
- Mindset liberation
- Freedom of speech
- Upping one's game with compassion and love for humanity,
  period

This book features business owners sharing their good-to-greatness
sentiments relative to their area of profession—the twists and turns of
consistently sourcing new levels of greatness in business and life. The
common denominator is that every single one of us continues to liberate
our mindset from constraining beliefs, experiences, and circumstances.
It's a lifelong adventure. The great news? Everyone reading this has
the capacity to do so. Surrounding yourself with a collective who will
champion, inform, and call you on your stuff when you are getting in
your own way is the way forward.

As business owners, the most influential liberation tool we have 100
percent control over is managing our mindset. Once understood, the

task is to consistently master one's thoughts for higher-vibration ones. This requires intentional engagement in commitments, conversations, and choices to forward focus, influencing freedom as we define it. This is "how" one's freedom experience unfolds and how the presence of greatness reveals itself—remarkable and unlimited.

We are not our thoughts! When we come to realize this, we become observers of our thoughts, and freedom ensues. An internal shift of responsiveness versus reaction then creates fresh, positive, external results.

Having worked with thousands of clients in individual and group settings, I've learned that the primary barrier between one's current circumstances and those striving to achieve resides between one's ears. Mindset combined with action (or the lack thereof) dictates what transpires next for us. The results you witness today are the perfect reflection of what your thoughts, actions, and behaviors were yesterday, last week, last month, etc. Sometimes looking in the mirror ain't too pretty. Other times, we're proud of who and what we see. Strive to be proud of your thoughts, actions, and behavior daily! Let go of circumstances no longer serving you, or perhaps never did. Let's focus on greatness.

Good to Greatness is a liberation campaign for business owners at all stages of growth. The vision? To collaborate with business owners—some you know and many you will meet—to influence individual and collective freedom for the highest good of all.

The world is in dire need to of flipping the incessant negative doom, gloom, division, and war spiel in all forms. Why drag this into the good-to-greatness liberation campaign?

- Because individual choices create a collective global energy for good or bad
- Because divisiveness only exists where relationships are fractured from conditioned societal pressure
- Because we can all agree that ostracizing, isolating, or banning those who have the conviction to not go along with what is mass dictated is clearly not serving us well

- Because love always conquers fear—haven't we had our fill of sensationalized fear mongering pushed upon us in recent times?
- Because we've lost sight of the value and power in community, starting with respect of one's neighbors, cities, regions, and nations regardless of differing perspectives
- Because we can be way better human beings with and to one another, right?

I wonder what our grandparents who fought in WWI and WWII would have to say?

The world is in the middle of an identity crisis. Understandably, many have numbed out for self-preservation due to the emotional toll experienced over the past few years. A multitude of storms reveal that perhaps things are not what we previously understood them to be. The need to preserve rights and freedoms our forefathers fought so hard to establish is apparent or risk the loss of them to globalism, a slow ascension in one direction or the other. Old systems are collapsing— some good and others . . . well, only time will tell. Division has many believing we are more different than alike. Societal conditioning is "how" we got here. How? If you tell someone something often enough, they will start to believe it.

Mainstream media IS societal conditioning—it's your choice to interpret what is fed to you as absolute truth or not. Not long ago, a presidential candidate ran his campaign focused on the immense "disinformation" taking place, which was met with criticism, rebuke, and judgment. Yet now, the term is socially accepted, utilized to express disdain, contradicting one's individual viewpoints. Who woulda thunk?

Everyone is in favor of free speech. Hardly a day passes without its being extolled, but some people's idea of it is that they are free to say what they like, but if anyone else says anything back, that is an outrage.

—*Winston Churchill*

Global economics is a messy puzzle with many missing pieces. It seems that many who govern have lost sight of currencies being backed by anything of value. Printing money for spending sprees at home and internationally looks more and more like a Monopoly game; quantitative easing is the norm versus the crisis exception it was intended for; election promises amnesia accepted as the norm; overreaching mandates for one's health and safety are now being questioned in the review mirror . . .

And so, a storm of divisiveness, economic strife, and distrust is our global crisis, an illusion that "they" know what's best for us so just follow along. This is what should be disconcerting to each of us as we consider voting with our purchases and rights in support of greatness for all moving forward. Liberation. Freedom. Greatness.

All the greatest things are simple, and many can be expressed in a single word: freedom; justice; honour; duty; mercy; hope.
—Winston Churchill

So, back to us as business owners collectively focusing forward in the spirit of greatness, creating one solution to shine enough light to thwart the darkness. Let's begin with leadership in our family, our circle of friends, our businesses, and then establish machines regionally, nationally, and internationally. The result? Liberation from limiting thought, behavior, and circumstances for all! Seemingly small changes can influence the quantum leaps of greatness of tomorrow.

If you want more greatness in your life experience, you've got to get out of your own way and go co-create it! Guess what? No one is coming to save you! Harsh? Well, truth isn't always comfortable, but it certainly can set you free. If we're to collectively experience expansive freedom, then liberation of self from the inside out is the starting point, which means becoming the leader of your own life.

Common traits of greatness in leadership involve:

- A positive, focus-forward mindset, no matter what perceived challenges exist
- Service in the highest good of all
- Results representing core values to enrich others' lives
- Efficiency to do less way better

- Honesty, transparency, 100 percent ownership when faced with less-than-desired results
- Ability to pivot to leave the negative and stumbles in the past
- Emotional intelligence
- Mindful conversations, commitments, congruency with words, choices, and actions
- Profit and prosperity principles
- Love versus fear

So, what can you expect to feel in an environment exuding greatness?

- A relaxed, mutually respectful, open-minded, lighthearted energy more often than not
- Differing perspectives understood as part of the human condition
- Zero tolerance for pettiness and low-level vibes
- A "work hard, play hard" energy
- Understanding that a reset to rest, regroup, and rejuvenate is a necessity, not laziness
- Empathy, compassion, and clear expectations to minimize assumptions
- Clear, consistent brand niche offerings to evolve through growth
- Consistent rewards for milestones achieved, small and large
- A reverence for money's use—its leverage-ability to liberate self and others

The gap between good and greatness is growth—individual, community, corporate, government. It starts with you getting clear on what greatness is, in the highest good for all. Many of us stop before we actually make the commitment to pursue greatness. Why? We're fixated on *how* before getting clear on *what* and *why*. The thing is, if we knew what the "hows" were, we'd already be living the desired greatness. The how is derived from the unwavering pursuit for our daily vision of greatness. Greatness requires changing our beliefs and circumstances, and so it can be a daunting prospect. It's easier to simply cancel ourselves out before someone else does or get comfortable being uncomfortable.

Perhaps we're all a tad weary from the past few years because we are too busy being in recovery mode. Have we defaulted into a mindset that to maintain is good enough? No judgment if that's the case. Topping up our reserves, literally and figuratively, is a primary need. Can we individually and collectively entertain and believe in greatness in ourselves, communities, corporations, and governments once again? This will challenge how we've thought and how things have been done up until now to reveal better ways to think, act, express, and lead. Is it uncomfortable and confrontational? Absolutely. Yet the flipside is worth the price of admission: greatness.

We can do this. It requires us to demand, expect, and nurture relationships of greatness on all levels—starting with the one between our ears! Putting our heads in the proverbial sand to say, "That's just the way it is," is how this storm gained momentum.

By reading this book, we, the contributors, want you to:

- Establish clarity on what a good life versus one of greatness will look and feel like for you.
- Identify what no longer serves you and deal with it, one proactive choice at a time.
- Engage in commitments, conversations, and choices that reflect belief in your greatness.
- Show up as an individual of greatness today, on every level.
- Speak your truth for what you believe around the global storms, no matter the backlash.
- Be 100 percent OK with others not aligning with your perspective; meet people where they are.
- Know your constitutional rights and have reverence for your grandparents' efforts.
- Choose love over fear every single day.

A few questions to consider that will maximize your reading experience:

- What will financial liberation in your business and personal life look like?
- What mindset belief no longer serves you that you go along with to maintain the status quo?
- If you innovate your own economy this year, what changes will you make?
- Consider the premise "no harm to life, liberty, or property"—how will you be a better human being this year?
- As a global citizen of Planet earth, how will you mindfully contribute to the healing of division?

Let's do this collectively.
Big love,
Christine and the rest of the contributors in this book

The Deeper the Why, the Deeper the Connection: Seven Steps to Ensuring Your Message Serves the Greater Good and Moves from Good to Greatness

Michelle Abraham

Henry David Thoreau, an American philosopher, naturalist, and author, once said, "Go confidently in the direction of your dreams; live the life you have imagined."

My parents chose that quote for me for my yearbook page the year I graduated. Little did I know the impact it would have on the way I live my life. After a tragic loss of a close friend at nineteen, while backpacking in Europe, I decided that life was too short, and I needed to make the most of the time I had on this planet. I took that message and my grief to heart, and for the next decade, my healing was finding the next adventure that fueled my soul.

I traveled on and off throughout my twenties. I experienced au pairing in Switzerland to sky diving in Mexico, scuba diving in Fiji, 4x4ing in Australia, bungee jumping in New Zealand, and sailing in the Whitsundays. I lived in ski resorts in Europe and Canada. I worked on cruise ships from Alaska to the Caribbean and from Panama to

Portugal. I led corporate groups and school kids on ski trips, kayaking and canoeing, rock climbing adventures, and ziplining. I was living my dreams. Forty-seven countries, a ton of credit-card debt, a worldly collection of friends, and incredible memories.

Living the life we have imagined for ourselves requires us to define what we truly want out of life. The life I had created, although incredible, was still lacking alignment and substance. It checked all the boxes in the freedom, fun, and adventure category, but it was missing something: a deeper reason. While the path to our dreams may not always be easy, we should never lose sight of our true heart's desire. I found myself longing for something more.

I went all over the world in pursuit of happiness and healing only to find that it was always there inside of me. I had gone confidently in the direction of my dreams, found the confidence to leap, taken risks, and never looked back or gave up on myself. I became comfortable being stretched out of my comfort zone. I said YES to me and YES to adventure. I believed in myself, yet the moment I stopped, slowed down, and turned inward for validation, love, and acceptance, I realized that I had everything I needed, wanted, or desired available to me—right here, right now. It was then that I met the love of my life and started to see what success was really like in other areas of my life and felt the deep sense of fulfillment. I stopped dreaming and settled for a great life.

We fell into "The American Dream": got married, bought a truck, a house in the suburbs, and had two kids. It was a great life, but to afford this great life, we had to sacrifice our happiness, work overtime, commute for hours, live for the weekends, rack up debt, and live stressed out. We would pass each other like strangers; as he came home from work, I would leave for work.

We had been talking for the last six months about moving from our current house in the city to his family's cabin on a lake on the Sunshine Coast of British Columbia so we could slow down a little, spend more time as a family closer to nature, and escape the craziness and stress of the city.

At 3:00 a.m. one morning we woke up to the sound of rushing water—a flood in our house. The flood caused so much damage that we had to move out for six weeks to an apartment the restoration company found for us. That flood forced us to finally listen to all those little voices and subtle signs that it was time for a change. I believe it was the universe's way of giving us a big kick in the butt for not having the courage to take steps toward a greater life. During those six weeks, we made the decision to list our house and see what might happen.

We had an offer in a few days. We were going to do it! My business, AmplifYou, was gaining momentum, and we could run it from anywhere. My husband quit his job of seventeen years, and we focused our energy on growing my podcast management business. We now happily run a high-six-figure company from an off-the-grid cabin on a lake. We take a boat to get to our car, and our kids take a boat to the school bus. And the best part of all, we only work with amazing people who have a big message to make a big impact in the world—from *The New York Times* bestselling authors to celebrities, doctors, TEDx speakers and everyday changemakers like you. We truly have created our own "American Dream" instead of following someone else's.

It hasn't always been easy, but I made a commitment to myself a long time ago. I vowed to only do work I love and use my voice to help others use their voice to make a difference and a positive impact in the world. Small, consistent action creates big changes over time. This may require taking risks and stepping outside of our comfort zones. However, by taking bold action and pursuing our passions, we can create a life that is fulfilling and meaningful on the journey from a great life to our even greater life—a constant leveling up!

Millions of people were awakened to a sense of unfulfillment in their mediocre lives during the COVID-19 pandemic. I have witnessed in many of my clients a longing for greatness and an urgency to get there—almost a feeling of making up for years of settling for less than.

Greatness is a moving target and an inspirational one that few of us will ever achieve, but the act of moving toward greatness is essentially the driving force. It is living a life beyond our dreams and society's expectations of settling and tuning into your own greatness.

Seven Steps to Greatness

We all have a story to tell, a story to inspire action, and one to make an impact on those who hear it. As a podcast producer, I have the privilege and honor to help thousands of stories be told and to celebrate our High Vibe Leaders who are making a huge impact in this world with their stories. The following seven steps create a deeper connection and are a manifesto for the journey to greatness.

1. **Get a BHAG (Big Hairy Audacious Goal):** When you set ambitious goals, you challenge yourself to go beyond what you think you are capable of.
2. **Pick your lane and put on your blinders:** Stay focused on your goals and stay in your lane to achieve them. Avoid the SOS (Shiny Object Syndrome) that plagues entrepreneurs and sabotages your focus.
3. **Fail fast and fail forward:** Embrace failure. You will inevitably encounter setbacks and challenges along the way, but it is important to embrace these setbacks and use them as opportunities to learn and grow, and the faster you can fall and get back up, the faster the path to greatness you stay on.
4. **Surround yourself with greatness.** It is said that you are the average of the five people you spend the most time with. If you want to achieve greatness, it is important to surround yourself with people who are also striving for greatness.
5. **Keep learning and growing.** You need to be willing to constantly learn new things, take on new challenges, and push yourself out of your comfort zone.
6. **Evolve out loud; start messy:** Use that message that's been on your heart and is dying to be heard; it will have an impact on the lives of others and give you a deeper why. It doesn't need perfection—it just needs to be heard.
7. **The deeper the why, the deeper the connection:** Find a purpose outside of yourself that's for the greater good in this world, a positive impact message to share. That's when you become unstoppable.

Moving from Good to Greatness means not settling for the status quo. Instead, tune in to your soul desire realignment and have the courage to go for it. Take imperfect action, start messy, share your voice, evolve out loud, and fail forward. Find your deeper why, keep growing, and surround yourself with others on this journey. We can and we will create a life beyond mediocre and step into the greatness we are meant to be.

Michelle Abraham
President / CEO

Podcast expert, Michelle Abraham is the founder of Amplifyou, described by Shark Tank alumni Kevin Harrington as North America's top podcast management company. Amplifyou specializes in helping visionary entrepreneurs make, market and monetize their podcasts while making a lasting impact. Michelle and her team have been nominated and won countless awards, having launched, managed 400+ podcasts in the last few years. Amplifyou operates on the values of authenticity, integrity and leading with service - working with entrepreneurs making a positive impact in the world.

michelle@amplifyou.ca
604-880-6599

What 'Good to Greatness' Means to Me!
Moving from Good to Greatness means not settling for the stat quo. Instead, tune into your soul's desire and go for it. Take imperfect action, start messy, share your voice, evolve out loud fail forward. In time, you too will go from Good to Greatness.

Podcasting; Message to Profit Roadmap
Ready to deliver and monetize your message through podcastin Your solution? Clarity, confidence, aligned messaging and coac to monetize your brand. The outcome? Launch a profitable podcast, be a profitable podcast guest with no wasted time, energy, money.

- Create your *Message to Money Visibility Roadmap*
- Be Media Ready; (Re)Align your business message
- Clarity for Podcast audience; done for you Media Sheet
- Curated list; 30 Podcasts to be a guest; booked on 2 sho in our network

Bonus:
- 2 Tickets to Podcast Success Blueprint 2-Day Event (virtual/in person)

Grab Your Podcast Success Blueprint Training
Valued $197

in f ⓞ

www.amplifyounetwork.com

Same Journey, Different Paths

Chris Adlparvar

Consider the flowers of a garden. Though differing in kind, color, form, and shape, yet, inasmuch as they are refreshed by the waters of one spring, revived by the breath of one wind, invigorated by the rays of one sun, this diversity increaseth their charm and addeth unto their beauty.
—'Abdu'l-Bahá

So, whose journey are you on? Is your journey the same as anyone else's? Can you love someone whose journey is different than yours? Have you cared for someone whose journey is different than yours? Could you accept someone whose journey is different than yours? The truth has always been that we are all the same. Philosophy, religion, and science have always said that, but in the quest for self-improvement, we have fallen into the trap of who is doing it better. In the end, we are all on the same journey—but on different paths.

For years when I was married to Erika, I always asked, "Why do I have to be first to heal my pains and fix my problems? Why shouldn't she do the work so I can just have my needs met? In many cases, the things I was asking for were valid and good. In some cases, they were even better for her as well. Yet, alas, as is the case with many other things, I had to change my thinking or approach before I could truly heal my life challenges.

Then there is my career. As we become more aware of the trauma we have had in life, we become more empathetic and caring of others, which can be very painful. Caring for those who have not started a healing process is usually harder because of their unwillingness to speak about the challenges of life from a perspective of self-awareness and self-empowerment. On top of that, we do not choose when to start a healing process. Seldom have I woken up and thought, *Today I will poke a bear and see how it goes.* Some trigger will come and find us. Whether the challenges of our children or our friends, the situation of the world, or some aspect of our energy levels, we will find that suddenly we are overwhelmed and cannot function properly.

If this is where you find yourself, you are now dysregulated—welcome to step one of healing. Now comes the work of identifying what has brought you here, what traumatic moments you've had, reliving those moments, making space for those emotions, separating the base emotions and your beliefs about those emotions, finding new understandings, forgiving, and loving, and interpreting things differently.

It is hard to be the person who suddenly understands how talking too much in a meeting makes it harder for others to participate. If like me, you are the extrovert, you're probably used to just saying everything that comes to mind, not realizing the impact it has on those who like to think a bit more before they talk. When I finally shut up, all I could hear were the other extrovert who hadn't learned to make space for others. The first option was to talk to them about it, but just telling them didn't help. Why was it that the same information that had changed me did not change them? What could I do to explain it better? Decades away from when I learned to listen better, I still struggle with our paths of learning. The truth is that it seems like we are all on a quest to learn about ourselves, our loved ones, our communities, our societies, and our histories, which means the learning has to be done repeatedly.

After a time, I could say, "I did all this healing work and changed in so many ways, but the world is still the same! Why can others not see it? If they were only willing to change, the world would be better place! Don't they care?" Then comes the thought that they may be bad people, which has provided justification for many an atrocity. Even worse, it has created the belief that people can be very different from one another. We may live different lives, but we are all are subject to the same basic forces.

Maybe you had to learn things in a way that was different than me. Maybe what worked for you will not work for me. Learning is not always efficient or linear. One of us cannot simply learn something and the rest of us know it. My parents knew things that would be best for me, but I insisted on learning them on my own, and so will my kids. After all, we have had fire around for millennia, and every generation still has to learn not to touch the stove. But why is this? Why would we need to relearn so much from generation to generation, from person to person?

We seem to require a creative process to help the growth of society. From the creation of a family or a business, we are always making new things. We can only create when we are willing to break what we already have, and this requires an openness to learn something new. Openness requires humility on our part toward life and an aspiration to discover that extends to being open to the way others live. I think we are all learning to create a wonderful life for ourselves and our loved ones.

We all require acceptance and support to learn. When we are in a relationship of safety and love, it is easier to see the impact of our own mistakes. Meanwhile, if we experience the fear of punishment, we become less willing to accept faults or look for new ways of doing things. In an extreme, we can start to believe that *we* are wrong instead of our behaviors having a negative impact.

While acceptance and support can be very helpful to the development of our communities, judgment and punishment are less effective in teaching and helping others grow. Reflect on the times when you learned the fastest. It will have been with those who loved you and made learning an easy task, almost play. You may not have many examples if you have had a rough life story, but even sweeter will be the memories of their smiles when you made mistakes, their voices, and the warmth of their embrace. When you calm your fears and sit with yourself, you come to know that love was always the way—and love has many more paths than you can imagine.

If we can understand the importance of acceptance in our own journey, it is easy to see how it will affect others. However, it can be very challenging to accept some perspectives if we are not willing to see people's attempt to create with the tools they have today.

In my limited experience of the entirety of human existence, what has taught me the most about acceptance is the curiosity to learn more about the paths others have had to take. The people who have been willing to share their inner difficulties with me have given me greater insight into my life and the world. Their courage and openness have also given me a lot more empathy and compassion. In fact, the more we share with one another, the closer we become.

Our life partners, for example, become so close to us because we can share the deepest parts of ourselves. Unfortunately, that does not mean they don't annoy us. The closer someone is to us, the more likely they can push our buttons. Our partners are likely to have somewhat similar life journeys, but there also will be areas of great difference. Our openness to get to know both sides is what brings us closer. In the same way, having time with those whose lives are very different from ours allows us a better understanding of our own life and purpose.

Our society is currently focusing more on the differences between us, to our detriment. With a sense of true curiosity and the required acceptance of what is, our view of the world becomes focused on the wonder we have to share with one another. So many of our fears are not well founded. As members of humanity, we have a lot more in common, and we all ask the same big questions. We are all concerned about our families and want to make the world better. We don't know how to do that and asking more questions about why we believe what we do will uncover the many similarities we have.

Our Splendour
businesses helping to make the world a better place

Chris Adlparvar
Consultant

Chris believes businesses play an important role in creating a better world for all. At Splendour, they help you align your business goals and operations to address your most pressing needs of community and, the world. Chris is a seasoned entrepreneur; six start-ups; 16+ years of experience in business strategy, operations, sales. He holds an Executive MBA candidate from Cornell and Queens Universities.

start@oursplendour.com
504-418-4137

What 'Good to Greatness' Means to Me!

As you develop as an individual, your business benefits too, literally moving from good to greatness. Then, your team becomes more invested in purpose and fulfillment. This translates into ease of attracting great, like-minded customers.

Splendour Operations Consulting

Learn to expand customer base, revenue streams, methodical operations for consistent brand recognition.

- Gain insight into key concerns of your community; develop essential solutions
- Preparedness; less viable products to validate needs to pivot quickly
- Identify what's worked to innovate and replicate it
- Nurture a team growth mindset; serve customers well
- Leadership growth; business is a reflection of you
- Build a team with open, honest communication for the needs of each individual

Price: Tailored Consulting Packages

Want to leverage biz for a better world?
Scan the QR code to book!

www.oursplendour.com

Back to Nature—YOUR Nature: An Inner Journey from Struggle to Ease

Monika Becker

Imagine you're holding a small seed in the palm of your hand. It contains the blueprint for a beautiful, majestic tree. Now, imagine you put the seed away. You do not plant it in the ground, you do not water it, and you deny it the love and care that would facilitate its growth into a big tree that has realized its potential. If you neglect the seed, the potential is still inside, but it remains unexpressed.

Now look at the unrealized potential in you. What are you doing with it? Have you nourished it in the past but lost motivation to bring more of it to light? Are you denying it the attention that would help it reach its full capacity? Do you feel there's more inside that you would like to express as part of YOU?

Is this you right now? Alive in some areas but dormant in others?

Would you prefer to feel like this? Alive in more dimensions with room to reach even more considerable heights and greatness?

Which tree would you like to be? How many more branches will you make alive on your tree? Which levels of YOUnique greatness will you reach?

In your business, not expressing your full potential may look like:

- Struggling and constantly comparing yourself to others who seem to be farther ahead and judging yourself for not having come as far
- Giving up on yourself and delaying your efforts to grow personally and professionally
- Minimizing your engagement behind default patterns that keep you stuck

Does any of this ring true for you? Are you sensing there's so much more of YOU to reveal, but you don't quite know how to access it? And are you afraid of staying stuck and wasting your life? Do you want to step into the fullness that is you?

Please know that you are not alone. Pain is part of life—for all of us. Pain is inevitable, but continuous struggle and suffering are optional. You do not have to stay stuck in struggle if you put in the effort and diligence needed to leave these troubles behind and move into ease and confidence. The decision is yours, and there is no wrong decision. Whatever you choose is your choice, and it's OK.

Greatness emerges when you turn inside to release your fears, insecurities, and inner conflict, see your full Self, and receive clear guidance from your inner intelligence. Greatness emerges when you rediscover and go back to YOUR nature!

Regardless of where you are in life and business right now, try to read the rest of my chapter with an open mind and heart. I will share a few of my experiences and ideas on how to express more potential and move from struggle to comfort, self-assurance, and greatness.

Looking at my life, I understand that we need to dig deep inside if we want to reach greater heights in the external world. "As within—so without . . ." In other words, to experience greater ease, confidence, impact, and joy in our lives, we must do a more thorough job at cleaning up our inner world to understand who we are and can be.

Perhaps you are asking, "Why do we even have to go back to our nature? Why are we no longer in touch with it?"

First and foremost, it's not your fault if you have lost connection to your true Self. Most of us lose touch with our true core by suppressing and negating parts of ourselves.

When we grow up, we are exposed to many different expectations, judgments, and established norms from families, friends, authority figures, and society at large. To be liked and feel secure, we tend to internalize these external influences and suppress thoughts and emotions that don't conform. This way, we end up living as "partial Selves" and drawing many detrimental and limiting conclusions about ourselves, others, and the world. As we continue to silence different aspects of our true selves, we slowly but surely lose the connection to our authentic nature—one repressed thought, emotion, or action at a time. While it may have been helpful to adapt and conform on these past occasions, this repressive way of thinking and behaving no longer serves us now.

Over time, our unexpressed thoughts and emotions accumulate unconsciously in our bodies and become energetic blockages. At some point, these energy blockages may cause mental, physical, emotional, or spiritual irritation, discomfort, fear, pain, and, in many cases, illness. Only when we come to a point when the pain gets too big, do we tend to pause and probe: "What's going on? What am I missing? Who am I and what's my life all about?"

I hit that kind of pain point in 2017. Intuitively, I knew that I had to work with my whole Self.

My default for problem-solving most of my life had been my logical mind. Thankfully, I had just been introduced to the Self-Healing Dalian Method. Its holistic nature made it the best and most effective tool for me at that time.

Working with the Dalian Method helped me dislodge the cobwebs of countless suppressed emotions, beliefs, assumptions, and judgments about myself and others that had piled up over decades of my life. My Dalian Method sessions reconnected me to my nature and gave me clarity about my genuine self and how to live with greater ease, self-trust, and strength. I also worked on clarifying my core values and using them as the guiding principles in my life. This inner work offered me a powerful way to reclaim my nature, unearth untapped potential within me, and live in alignment with what matters to me most at my core. Life and business have changed for me! If I can do it, so can you!

Yes, it is totally possible to reconnect to those dormant parts of yourself that may feel lost from you. As it was for me, it's possible for YOU to regain the confidence, creativity, and joy of living your true Self, YOUR nature, and release it into the world.

While intellect is amazingly helpful in making sense of our insights, our logical mind will never be able to identify the root causes hidden in our unconscious that create struggle. It is through the wisdom of our body, emotions, and spirit that we can lift ourselves up and nourish the neglected seed of greatness living inside each of us. I encourage you to find the approach or tool that works for you. The Dalian Method was and still is transformative and empowering for me, but it may be something else that resonates with you. Research can help you find the avenue that speaks to you. Choose what's best for you, and then get started on your inner work. That effort was so worth it for me!

One closing point: Remember that you are not living in isolation. As a human being and business owner, you are part of a community that you influence through your unique presence and contribution. If you hold back, you deprive your community of your special energy and unique gifts. However, when you elevate yourself, you expand the space for others to rise to greater heights as well.

Just imagine the powerful ripple effect you may create by stepping into your greatness and opening the space for others to join you in embracing their own potential. Business leaders just like you have the power to change our world for the better, one confident leader and one ripple at a time. So please don't deny the rest of us all the parts of YOUR nature!

Know that your greatness is possible, our world needs it, you deserve it, and I'm here to support your growth from tiny seed to towering tree. So, be great at being all of YOU!

It's an all-around win for you, your business, and our world.

Marianne Williamson, American author, spiritual leader, and political activist, put it so well in her book *A Return to Love*:

Our deepest fear is not that we are inadequate. Our deepest fear is that we are powerful beyond measure. It is our light, not our darkness, that most frightens us. We ask ourselves, who am I to be brilliant, gorgeous, talented, fabulous? Actually, who are you not to be? You are a child of God. Your playing small doesn't serve the world. There's nothing enlightened about shrinking so that other people won't feel insecure around you. We are all meant to shine, as children do. As we're liberated from our own fear, our presence automatically liberates others.

Monika Becker
Owner

From a young age, Monika supported the people in her life as an attentive listener, problem-solver, and confidante. After her layoff from a corporate job in 2008, she decided to take coach training and turn her natural talents into her profession. Monika now helps leaders become better leaders - all from the inside. Her motto "Back to YOUR Nature!" exemplifies the need to rekindle their inner landscape so they can lead with ease and impact.

monika@cleardirections.ca
+1 (604) 816-4056

What 'Good to Greatness' Means to Me!

Greatness emerges when I turn my focus inside to release m
fears, insecurities, and inner conflict, and I receive clear guid
from my inner intelligence. Also, I need to live by my core val
and connect to a sense of purpose for motivation and inspira
along the way.

Back-to-YOUR-Nature Leadership Boo

A 6-week online group program to help you get back to YOU
nature, gain a clear sense of self, and grow your ability to live
lead with ease, authentic strength, and confidence.

What you will get:
- *Leader Strength Self-Assessment* to identify where yo
  at right now.
- *Processes to explore* your core values, purpose, and
  vision.
- *Exercises to quiet your mind* and receive guidance fro
  your inner intelligence.
- *Action plan template,* customizable to match YOUR
  nature.
- *Private Facebook group* for support between sessions

Book your complimentary 45-minute Clarity Sessi

Valued at $195

in f ⓘ

www.cleardirections.ca

Take Your Finances from Good to Greatness

Gwen Do

If you fail to plan, you are planning to fail.

—Benjamin Franklin

This quote by Benjamin Franklin holds true in many aspects of life, including your wealth. Those who design even a simple financial plan with a date and dollar-specific value have a much greater chance of building and preserving wealth than those who don't. The absence of a financial plan is often accompanied by a lack of awareness as to what a realistic financial goal is or how to achieve it, and thus leads to limited action toward reaching that goal.

Financial empowerment is not a measure of net worth. It just means having the confidence and ability to control your money versus letting your money control you, regardless of how much money you have. A lack of financial control can be paralyzing, especially to those in vulnerable positions.

Women, for example, are on average less confident than men in their ability to manage their finances. For many, financial empowerment is life-altering. When you have your finances under control, the effects extend to other areas of your life, helping you to achieve your dreams. As a woman growing up in a traditional Vietnamese family, I never learned about finances, so I can relate to the struggle that many women have when it comes to money.

Today, I help women by providing the tools they need to take command of their financial futures and establish financial empowerment. I suggest the following eight recommendations:

1. **Improve your financial literacy.** Education unlocks a multitude of possibilities. To manage your money well, you need a basic understanding of the principles of budgeting, borrowing, and investing. You should also understand how interest rates affect the cost of borrowing and how compounded growth can help you build wealth.

2. **Check your credit score regularly.** Your credit score is a value primarily based on your prior payment history and the amount of debt you carry. This score is used by lenders to determine how much to charge you for borrowing money. If your credit score is low, you can expect to pay a higher interest rate for car loans, home mortgages, and credit cards. Paying bills on time and decreasing your debts can improve your score and help you save money.

3. **Understand that not all debts are equal.** Not all debts are the same. Mortgages and student loans, which are tied to a potentially appreciating asset, are generally considered to be "good debt," while high-interest credit-card balances are generally considered to be "bad debt."

4. **Plan for retirement.** If you want to retire on time with enough money to maintain your desired lifestyle, the earlier you start planning and saving, the better. A simple planning session to determine how much money you will need to live and how much you should save regularly will go a long way toward actualizing your goals. While the amount you need to save may look daunting, there are many strategies that can be adapted to any situation.

5. **Plan for the unexpected.** Life is always full of surprises—and unfortunately, some surprises can be expensive. Cars break down, hot water tanks burst, and teeth chip unexpectedly. Setting aside an emergency fund will provide you with peace of mind and help you deal with the unforeseen. Choose an amount that will cover your lifestyle and allow for mishaps, and once you have that amount set aside, continue to save for your other goals. Most experts recommend

setting aside three to six months' worth of living expenses (not income) in a liquid, interest-bearing savings account.

6. **Create a spending plan and a budget.** If you are spending more than you earn, you will never get ahead—in fact, it's a sure sign that your finances are headed for trouble. The best way to make sure that your income is greater than your expenses is to track your expenses for a month or two and then create a budget.

7. **Protect your biggest asset—your ability to earn an income.** Income protection insurance will protect you for the length of time you are unable to work, and depending on your occupation, if you are unable to return to work, payments continue until age sixty-five. In addition to protecting you, income protection protects those who are dependent on you, allowing you to provide for them if you are unable to work.

8. **Improve your money mindset.** What you do with your money is important. But how you think about it can be important too. Your thoughts can influence your actions. When applied to your finances, your core beliefs about money and your money mindset will influence how you save, spend, and manage debt.

The definition of financial success is different for everybody and depends on your own desired outcomes. Taking your personal finance from good to greatness requires discipline and consistency. It's just like training for a marathon—it won't happen overnight. The key is getting started and gradually taking small steps toward your financial goals. If you want results, you must be willing to get uncomfortable because that's where growth happens.

Regardless of your goals, I hope these recommendations will help you on your own financial journey. Remember, you don't have to be on this journey alone. Talk with those whom you love and experts whom you trust, and they will help you along the way.

SmartPlan Financial

Most people don't plan to fail, they just fail to plan.

Gwen Do
Founder

Gwen's passion and openness helps her get to know her clients on a deep, personal level to learn about their dreams, desires, and drives. This intimacy enables authentic relationships while helping clients to reach their financial goals. Gwen strongly believes that no matter where you are in life, you can always build progressively towards achieving bigger and bigger goals. In her spare time, she leads an active life playing tennis, volleyball, and is currently training for her first half marathon.

gwen.do@smartplanfinancial.ca
778-892-6445

in ◎

www.smartplanfinancial.ca

What 'Good to Greatness' Means to Me!

For most people, money is necessary for survival; it is the medium we use to acquire the food we eat, the clothes that we wear, and the homes that we live in. Transitioning from good to greatness means having and acting on a personalized financial plan to fully maximize ones earning potential. Rather than earning enough to survive, greatness means having the financial freedom to pursue our dreams, enjoy the luxuries of life, protect your loved ones, and secure our retirements.

Financial Wealth Assessment

Ready to witness safety, security and momentum in your wealth building? Our financial wealth assessment is your first step.

- Understand your current financial situation to create a future wealth vision
- Uncover what is getting in your way of witnessing momentum
- Discover the various financial strategies and solutions available to you
- Receive personalized wealth options no matter your current status
- Work with a woman in business who understands what women need
- Receive a complimentary wealth assessment

Scan Here for Your Complimentary Financial Assessment

The Lore of Acquisition

Ruth Elisabeth

It is fascinating to ponder the foundations of my lived experience over the last thirty-five years in terms of *Good to Greatness* in business. My first small business, at age twenty as a young nurse, employed three medical teams to administer cholesterol tests within the community through pharmaceutical outlets. I wrote the resources, calibrated the equipment, rostered medical staff, set up their locations, and went to the beach for the day. At the end of the day, I would pull down the teams, take the cash, and go out for dinner. This ended eight months later, as it was a short-lived social fad. This experience left me with a strong sense of failure as cash flow subsided, staff were let go, and overheads still needed to be addressed.

My second enterprise involved a team of photographers, sales staff, and telemarketers who operated both city and remote country regions in family portraiture. I was twenty-five years old and loved this business. I had the freedom to travel and explore, always my favorite thing to do in all work ventures. Two years and a few hundred thousand dollars later, the printer moved the business house over an extended time, which collated into the biggest failure of my life as cash flow stopped and I opted for bankruptcy.

WHY? An underlying secret that I hid away was that I was broken from earlier abuse, which left me with a nervous breakdown every six months. I was a borderline alcoholic and definitely a workaholic at the age of twenty. Many secrets longed to be heard, but I was petrified to be loved. Instead, I sought approval, as proving success was my only target to self-worth. My life was driven by the fear of exposure and fully compartmentalized. I worked hard to hold myself together with a high external performance, but I kept myself isolated from others.

My inner foundation had to change. I had to heal my past to create my future. A question came to mind one day: "Would you put a wounded child on your board of directors?" NO! Everything suddenly made sense! My wounded child *imprinted* every quantum creation.

Today, I train with my signature DIAMOND QUANTUM SCHOOL, so my students can identify as Quantum Creators. Hidden foundational wisdom must be understood to thrive as a successful creator in business or entrepreneurial endeavors.

Identity

My first question to a new client is always, "If your Soul pulled out of the top of your head right now, what would your body do?" It would fall on the ground. Yes! Simple, perfect science. Your doctor knows it. Your lawyer knows it. Scientists know it. Your Uber driver knows it. Everyone knows it. You know it.

So, it is your *Soul* that keeps you upright on your feet! If you ask most people if they have studied the science of the Soul, most will say no. Most only focus on physical body wellness. Yet you are made up of a physical, emotional, mental, and spiritual body, and *genius* is your very own energetic signature and unique makeup. You are *energy in motion* sparking in and out of sight in this third dimensional plane. You are your Soul who wrote your life script before you came here. That is what déjà vu is. You are a Creator. You came from Light, you *are* Light, and you expand as Light into your next creation.

Quantum Field

Imagine the quantum field like a still glassy lake out in front of you without a ripple. Every thought, feeling, and desire cast onto your quantum field ripples back to you every descriptive vibration projected out from yourself exactly as you cast it. The quantum field is the primordial way all things of Creation manifest. It has no bias or judgment of good or bad, justice or injustice. Just you and your thoughts, feelings, beliefs, values, and prior influences that reverberate in *every second* are emanations that must draw response. That must create and be returned into your lived experience. Your quantum field is inside your body within your DNA. So, your absolute inner world must show up in your outer world. We are Creators of worlds. A quantum principle is *Energy goes where you intend it to flow.*

The Lore of Acquisition

"Lore of Acquisition" are words I heard upon waking seven years ago. Spooky! Two years of experiential living brought my study together to the height, depth, and breadth of the Lore of Acquisition and how manifest Creation works. It is insanely brilliant. Follow along with me on this.

After an excruciating client session when she simply was not "getting" it, I threw my hands in the air and yelled, "What is it with her?"

My Soul said:

"A conqueror needs a battle to overcome; a victor has the gates open before them."

We continuously create on our quantum field, but one creation is opulent, and the other is built in survival and struggle. I call this Plan A and Plan B creating. The *CONQUEROR creator* creates difficulty and hardship to continuously overcome. The *VICTOR Creator* has exquisite flow; opportunities and invitations pour in. A worthy contemplation: which Creator are you? What would you prefer? Oh, sweet recognition! Yes, let's change that right now!

My first job is to connect you with your Soul Self! My second job is to show you how this works by the Lore of Acquisition as a Creator and how to change it. As a Living Creator, I like to break up our creations into percentages to prove results in business acquisition and the level of *acquisition* in which you are operating today. Your potency, when aligned with your Soul, is 100 percent Creation where everything flows in full circle to the attainment of you LIVING your Creation.

Your little pointy you, the often wounded you, is usually producing about 3 percent of a Creation when not connected energetically with your Soul Source. So, you pixelate a great plan or idea with new partners, feel thrilled, but then it falls apart or de-pixelates, only to suffer loss instead of gain. This is one of many indicators showing which *Creator* you are creating from, the conqueror or the victor.

How is your life evolving for you?

Visualization

Place yourself into the center of a round room of thirty red doors. It is red door after red door after red door. Take your time. Feel or see how many red doors are open.

That number of open doors is your Lore of Acquisition *as a Creator proved* and directly explains your receivability. Now open all the red doors and feel the quantum possibilities to allow creation to flow in!

Most business owners only have one or two red doors open as *Creation Streams.* Only two places from which to receive money. Some innovators surprisingly have no doors open; some may have three to six.

Your direct physical, spiritual, emotional, and mental body beliefs pinch off your Lore of Acquisition as a Creator. Your little pointy you, or your alter ego, must comprehend your identity as a Living Creator and your vast ability to create, heal, and manifest. Imagine receiving from everywhere!

Self-appraise your business. Feel your Lore of Acquisition story as I introduce each concept:

- Time/Labor
- Time/Luxury
- Serving/Living
- Love people/Like Isolation
- Dollars/Luxury
- Love/Hate marketing

- Commitment/Trust
- Fair/Unfair
- Survival/Success

What is your vibrational quantum feeling story when I mention your vehicle, travel, love, relationship, financial systems, money, or food? Your body, your health?

Observe that in a split second, *you Creation-Wrapped* each of these! A Lore of Acquisition that *must* be your outcome according to your own projection, vibration for vibration. For each topic you gave a fleeting opinion, a reason, or a degree of difficulty, and a time/space law as to how and when to get your stuff. The why, when, where, and how! You laid a "little you" *human law* construct around it, *limitation*, and by the Universal Lore of Acquisition, SO IT IS!

What services are you delivering? Is it aligned with your Soul path and feels right for you? What are you Creating and why?

Beliefs and Values

As an entrepreneur, what do you instinctually jump to with your beliefs and values? What have you been taught? These are creation matrices which hold your vibrational world hostage. *These are not blocks; they are direct creations.*

As an example, I loved the quality of *endurance* and was proud of my resilience to overcome. Yet if endurance is being put onto my quantum field, then what is going to return to me? More to endure! Simple. You are falsely taught to be a warrior—to push through, set goals to achieve pittance in the future and set affirmations while disconnected from your Soul. No! You are the Creator, and if you believe this, you will create more direct hardship into your future, pushing your success away. Hidden *vibrational story creations* hold us ransom from receiving all we dream of.

You can learn to remove large, hidden stories in sequential order and connect to your Soul, where you can create joyfully and deliberately. As business builders with a big heart for others, we want freedom for all; however, we must attend to ourselves first. Devolve ourselves of the past so that we can opulently Create our futures by the LORE OF ACQUISITION.

You are a Creator right here and now. Let's heal the wounded child and create without limitation. SO IT IS.

Diamond Matrix Masters
Immense Value for Precious Little

Ruth Elisabeth
Author and Public Speaker

Ruth is a dynamic and passionate teacher and healer bringing Souls alive. With guided knowledge and much humor Ruth trains in her masterclasses and signature school the DIAMOND QUANTUM SCHOOL.

Her own Soul journey evolved into a powerful series of energetic light body activations which truly integrates souls to their purpose.

Ruth's understanding of Quantum Lore guides others to understand how creation works and how to operate from Soul Sovereignty.

250 927 0388
diamondmatrixmasters@gmail.com

in 𝕏 ⓞ f
www.diamondmatrixmasters.net

What 'Good to Greatness' Means to Me!

My Soul mission was to learn my Identity and my innate quantum abilities. I learned the difference between vibrational human law constructs to creating versus the true Quantum Lore; to flip my life from broken to Creating. Quantum Lore is absolute and ignites from the Creator inside each of us.

As a public speaker and author I love to bring others into their Soul connection and train them in accelerated Quantum Lore to now Create.

Aura, Light Body Session

People arrive with fractional symptoms that can take years to explore and consolidate into healing. The 90-minute session drastically reduces one's healing time with powerful bio energetic activations to experience physical, emotional, mental and spiritual body alignment. This is the first DIAMOND QUANTUM SCHOOL Session.

Your 90-minute Session:
- Clears head for mental function and clarity to flow
- Brain chemistry rebalance
- Heals your central nervous system and meridian system
- Clears physical body systems
- Set up your Auric field and Light Body

Aura, Light Body Session - 90-Minute $250

Scan QR code to book

Going from Good to Great, Inside and Out

Rachel Gooen, MS, MSW, LCSW

What helped me take my consulting business from good to great? Well, that's a pretty funny question since I constantly wonder if I'm good, much less great. But that's quite normal. Our brains are designed for negativity, so it's easy to believe that we aren't doing our best. And it doesn't help when many of us work for ourselves and don't have a team to reflect the wins.

So how could I evaluate myself?

I could measure:

- The amount of money I brought in
- The amount of people on my client list
- The amount of money I'd saved for retirement
- The number of days I spent on vacation
- Everything I could buy without taking out a loan

All fine measures, but only if material gain and what it brought me was what mattered most. There are lots of ways to make money, but they only told one part of my story. What I was really striving for was to be the best practitioner I possibly could be. To be doing my "craft" of facilitation, training, and mentoring well and helping my clients become their best.

I wanted to feel 100 percent authentic, confident, and at ease on the job so my clients could feel that way, too.

So, What Was Missing?

To external observers, I was already a highly qualified and successful consultant with two master's degrees and twenty years of experience, yet while people told me I was skilled, I vacillated in my confidence. I had plenty of education and experience, but I felt like I was either falling short of my highest potential or achieving it only when I felt total trust and comfort with the person or group I was working with. Well, that wasn't OK with me!

When I stepped back and engaged in honest self-evaluation, I realized I had all the tools, skills, and knowledge I needed, along with a successful career.

What was missing was *bravery* and *inner strength* to share my abilities in all situations.

Taking Inventory

Being a good facilitator of conversations means realizing that you yourself are the "tool" that helps people converse. You keenly notice what everyone in the room is feeling and thinking, and then make an inventory of their reactions. Are participants understanding one another, reacting to one another, and able to listen to one another? Or are they distant, distracted, and focused only on delivering their own opinion, viewpoint, or solution?

Every person learns differently, communicates differently, and comes to a conversation with different preconceived ideas due to their personal history and cognitive abilities. As a facilitator, my greatest skill was the ability to first understand myself and my personal reactions to everyone else in the room and their comments and interactions with others, and then assess if how I perceived things was due to my own personal history and cognitive abilities or these other people's characteristics.

To hone this skill, I practiced mind-focusing in many forms, such as daily extended sitting meditations, shorter regular mindfulness check-ins, and introspective activities like journaling. Little by little, I taught myself to notice what I was thinking and feeling in the moment whenever someone said something. Then I'd ask, "Why does this statement bring that to mind or make me feel this way?"

What others called insight, intuition, or the ability to "read the room" began with first learning to "read" myself.

Becoming Brave and Strong

Taking inventory of myself taught me that we rarely know what people really mean when they say something. That's when bravery came into play. I had to be brave enough to ask if my understanding of what they said was in fact what they meant. I had to be strong and self-aware enough to feel my feelings, even when they aren't always nice feelings, and strong and self-aware enough again to observe my mind without believing every thought I had.

What was true for me was true for everyone else in the room. For years, I could see when two people were misunderstanding each other or not taking the time to listen for understanding, but I wasn't brave enough to skillfully point that out to them. I just facilitated the conversation and hoped that they would either notice or not notice, and then work out the misunderstandings later rather than in the present moment when I could assist. I could feel the tension, or feel the pain, or feel the confusion, but I would just think, *I'm not sure I should say something.*

Well, here's what I finally figured out: If I was feeling it . . . *everyone* was feeling it.

Now I know that facilitating well also means speaking up. Part of being a good mentor, coach, therapist, or facilitator is helping others engage with themselves and one another. It's not giving advice or leading, but rather stepping in and making the process easier; it's reflecting back to people whatever it is I see happening and offering helpful tools to reduce conflict and strengthen creativity and connection—including the internal connections clients feel within themselves.

From Facilitating to Transforming

When I brought the strength and bravery of self-reflection and self-expression into my work, what was when facilitative became transformative. My business started to really become meaningful and the experience for everyone went from good to great.

As one client, an executive director of a nonprofit, said:

> *I think the biggest thing your coaching has helped me with is building my confidence. When I started, I was in survival mode. I was happy in my job, but I felt like I couldn't mess things up. I was on the edge of everything. I was reactionary. I felt pressure to respond to everyone. I now feel like I can take a deep breath.*
>
> *Your coaching has taught me to say, "What do you want your response to be? Who do you want to be on the other side of the response? What do you want the quality of the response to be so you can give it the response you want to make?"*
>
> *I've learned how to prioritize what I need to make this role better for me so I'll stay in it. Your coaching did such a great job of teaching me how to use self-reflection.*
>
> *Previously I felt so fragile, and now, due to our conversations, I feel more confident with who I am in the organization and with myself as a leader. I think it is due to our conversations.*

Getting testimonials like this doesn't stop my drive for self-improvement. But they remind me that change, like trust, begins within. If I want to keep making my consultant practice better, I have to keep being brave and strong in how I assess and express myself, and then invite clients to do the same.

rachel gooen consulting
an outside ear to help you navigate the intricacies of leading a team

rachel gooen

Rachel loves people! She's guided by a deep interest in healthy work cultures, helping leaders shift team behaviors and mindsets. For the past 15 years, she's refined her knowledge and skills in guiding organizations through positive change. How? By asking the right questions, listening deeply and cultivating a culture of belonging. In the end change is never easy, but through deep engagement and a little bit of fun, she can help you thrive as a leader.

Rachel@rachelgooen.com
406-360-7685

what 'good to greatness' means to me!
It takes bravery, vulnerability and a willingness to ask for help. My work shifted from good to great when I started "putting myself out there", leaned into my strengths, then created the right support team to go for goals of greatness!

your deep dive change
All sessions held on zoom (in person in Missoula, MT)

1:1 Coaching: (3 / 6 / 9 / 12-month packages)
- Tailored to your specific objectives for positive, measurable change;
- Gain Greater awareness of impact on others
- Greater resilience, clarity and effectiveness
- Improved thinking capacity under pressure
- Improved leadership & team engagement

Choose a focus:
- Balancing demands of work and life
- Navigating Complexity & Challenges
- Nurturing Culture & Teams
- Resilience / Managing Self
- Leading through Crisis or Change
- Boosting Confidence and Belief
- Play to your Strengths

Complimentary Deep Dive Coaching Session - 45 minutes
VALUE $175
Scan QR code to book!

FACILITATOR · TRAINER · COACH

in

www.rachelgooen.com

A Man Is Not a Financial Plan

Margaret Johnson

Whether you're single or married, life is much more complicated now than it was in your mother's day. A woman's relationship with money is more diverse and complex than ever before. Women are no longer housewives or stay-at-home moms being taken care of by their husbands. Instead, we are CEOs and the presidents of companies, and we have learned that we can be anything we want to be. Gone are the days you must depend on a man to be your financial plan.

Financial Greatness Is Yours to Claim

It's all up to you. No matter what your current relationship status might be, you will likely be handling money on your own at some point in your life—accepting responsibility for your life, taking care of yourself, and growing your business. When it comes to money, procrastination is a common obstacle, especially for women. For women, procrastination usually comes from fear, not laziness. Many women avoid taking control of their finances because they're afraid they'll fail, which means everyone will be disappointed. Other women are afraid of succeeding because of the responsibility having money entails. Overcoming these fears is critical to ensuring your financial security and your future.

Your net worth does not measure your self-worth. There is no question that money is a supercharged topic. So, when it comes to your relationship with money, change doesn't happen overnight, especially when discussing traits and habits that have become embedded in your character thanks to years and years of practice. Your family history and feelings of self-worth are all tied up in your ability to make a living, support your family, get ahead in your career, and in some cases, start your business.

For many of us, values serve as our internal compass. Unfortunately, keeping our values at the forefront with all the world's distractions is tough; they get buried beneath the expectations and values of others. The weight of social conformity, false beliefs, and even some of the messages and lessons we've learned during our upbringing factor in. It's a lot to think about.

But when our behavior is consistent with our values, we feel contentment, satisfaction, and internal strength. Conversely, when our behavior is misaligned with our values, we feel lethargic, depressed, and frustrated—even angry and without purpose . . . especially when it comes to money.

Therefore, it is critical to learn about finances and know what to do and when. How you understand and use money determines your ability to bring your dreams to life.

Success Is Not a Four-Letter Word

One of the greatest lessons I learned after years of being in business is that there are two ways of thinking. You can believe there is more than enough business to go around (the abundance mindset)—or you can believe there is not (the scarcity mentality).

Either way, you are right.

I spent countless years thinking that "everyone" knew more than I did and that everyone was my competition. This constant "competition" left me paralyzed, unable to move ahead, stressed, and never feeling good enough.

I took course after course, hoping to discover what I thought I didn't know about business, and I hired countless "professionals" to help me—all to no avail. Finally, I began to understand that my thinking was all wrong. No one knows more about being in business than I do. It is 100 percent up to me to create my desires.

In 1999 I created Solutions Credit Counselling Service Inc. Five years later, our gross revenue was over $1,000,000; the next year, it was even higher. In 2001, Women and Money Inc. came to life—I created another successful company.

So, I *do* know a lot about business!

And one thing I am sure of is that there is enough business to go around. In fact, there is *more* than enough. There is enough money, enough business, and enough opportunity for all of us to live abundantly. When you begin to embrace that belief, you will see it manifest in your business and in your life. Instead of fearing and fighting the power of money, we need to manage it better, channel it, and use it to change the world for good. When you focus on service to others, the money always follows.

It's more than money; it's your life!

Women and Money Inc. isn't about helping women to merely financially survive. It's about a conviction to see all women financially *thrive*. It marries my passionate vision, my dreams for women to understand their rights and responsibilities regarding their money—to leverage what they have to create what they want, not just need. Many women think they aren't good with money. But what they really mean to say is that they don't know how to use money. How do you know what you don't know? We provide solutions for this piece.

We are on a mission to support women and women entrepreneurs in one of the most important parts of their life and business: money. The entrepreneurial path is not for the faint of heart or the financially inept. But with the appropriate financial knowledge and skills, you can and will elevate your business and live the dream life you crave.

Money Mindset—Rewrite Your Money Story

Wealth is not a four-letter word. However, for many women, money avoidance is a real thing. While highly motivated in other areas of our lives, many of us drag our feet regarding financial issues.

As an entrepreneur, your money mindset is the key to financial liberation; it's your most powerful financial asset. Once we can see our money and where we stand financially, we can make better choices. Therefore, when we make it visual, and when we can measure what our money is doing or not doing, it then becomes easier for us to make the best financial decisions for us and our businesses.

Life Feels Better

Life—both our personal life and our work life—feels better when we are in control of our money. One of the biggest myths in business is that a profitable company can't go bankrupt. They can, and they do. Why? Because they don't pay attention to what their financial information tells them.

Your life goals depend on your business and its success.
So how do you get started for success?

1. Get crystal clear on what matters in your life.
2. Identify your personal life goals.
3. Identify your business goals.
4. Learn how to read and understand your financial statements.
5. Know your financial position and that of your business.
6. Pay your taxes and bills on time all the time.

Your financial statement is your best decision-making tool. It tells you where you are, where you've been, and where you are going.

Financial statements are your best friends. Learn to love them!
One of the biggest fears for entrepreneurs is running out of money. However, when you are on top of your financial statements, you can predict the future.

Financial statements consist of three interconnected statements:

- The balance sheets
- The profit and loss statement
- The cash flow statement

Together they tell the story of every financial business decision you make.

Remember, profit is more than putting money in the bank: Profit = Revenue – Expenses – Taxes $$$. There are three different types of profit:

1. Gross Profit
2. Operating Profit
3. Net Profit

Finally, remember that cash is king—it's the lifeline of your business!

Create a Successful Money Story

To create a successful money story for you and your business, you need to:

- Identify your current financial situation, both personal and business.
- Reflect on the past to find out where you've been.
- Use the past information to plan your future.
- Set some goals for where you want to go.
- Set personal goals before setting business goals.
- Monitor your progress weekly and stay on track.

Your money beliefs appear in every financial decision, including how you finance your company. Stop putting your head in the sand. Start knowing your numbers. Business grows by design, not by default. You can't manage what you don't measure. Knowing your numbers and making data-driven decisions accelerates your business growth, increases profitability, and helps you to make better decisions about what to focus your time on.

The more focused you are on your time, energy, and money, the more money you can keep, and the more you can increase your productivity, results, and self-worth. Focus on these things:

- Your gross revenue
- Your expenses

- Your profit margin
- Your average revenue and lifetime revenue per client
- Your customer attrition rate and conversion rates
- Your client acquisition cost
- The number of leads
- The frequency of sales activities
- Your highest return on investment
- Your best-performing lead generation to date

Financial liberation is not a destination; it's an active state of being. In other words, you must always keep on top of your finances. No more depending on a man to be your financial plan—you can write a better money story and thrive in all areas!

The road to success is always under construction.
—Lily Tomlin, actress, comedian, writer, and producer

Women and Money Inc.
A Man Is Not a Financial Plan
Solving Your Money Puzzle™

Margaret Johnson
President & CEO

Margaret was nominated twice for Entrepreneur of the Year. She is a thought leader in the field of financial counselling and education. In 1999 she started Solutions™ Credit Counselling Service Inc. In 2001 she created Women and Money Inc. to help women understand personal and business finance - a life passion. Margaret is an Insolvency Counsellor registered by Industry Canada, President of The Canadian Association of Independent Credit Counselling Agencies, and a distinguished public speaker, educator, and writer.

mhjohnson@womenandmoney.com
604 580 4079

WHAT 'GOOD TO GREATNESS' MEANS TO ME!

Good to Greatness means doing more with less and getting better results while having the courage to stay true to me and my beliefs.

YOUR PROFIT PLAN PROGRAM / LIMITED SPOTS

Commit to realizing profit in your business. This program helps you; discover where you are financially; how to establish proven profit formula now; easy to implement plan that works. "It's not about the money, it's all about the money." Let's get you from revenue to profit, now.

- 3 x 45-minute online group sessions (recorded)
- Templates provided for each session steps
- Each session includes Q+A time to receive solutions for your specific circumstances

Session I: Revenue for Profit Formula + Inventory
Session II: Expenses + Debt to Profit
Session III: Profit Allocation Formula to Scale

Price $489 CAN or $280 x 2

BOOK 30 MIN CALL

in f

www.womenandmoney.com

Turning Fear into Love

Maggie Judge and Marla Ulstad

I am in the right place at the right time, doing the right thing.
—Louise Hay

I adjust the rearview mirror and gaze at my reflection. The sun is shining in the side window, warming my face. I seem to have a glow that I haven't noticed in a long time, and I'm smiling from every square inch of me. I take a deep breath in and an even deeper breath out. I laugh out loud . . . excited and in disbelief. For two years, I have returned to my car after each oncology appointment, taking a breath and sitting to reflect on the update that I will later recount to my husband and daughter. Every detail is captured in my notes, but today the conversation is vividly replaying in my head as I sit here.

"Maggie, you are not in remission . . . you are cancer-free."

What a gift! I feel overwhelmed with gratitude. And my journey isn't over—healing is something that is more than just physical; it goes deep and extends way beyond my cancer.

After an unexpected breast cancer diagnosis in November 2020, every one of my previously held beliefs, values, habits, and routines had to be reevaluated. Fear can creep into every aspect of a cancer diagnosis— from the cancer itself, to the treatment plan, to navigating the many changes and unknowns. It is overwhelming to the nervous system. This is not a healthy state to be in. I had to find a way to shift from this state of fear to something that was more conducive to healing and that supported my body through this. I started to realize that cancer was a wake-up call: It was happening FOR me, not TO me. My body was making it clear that I was here in this moment to learn something.

Fear is an alarm. It signals us to check in and see if we are in danger or about to experience pain. What did I fear before my cancer diagnosis? Well, being enough and feeling worthy of others' love and approval were just a few. I was hustling through life with an unhealthy focus on producing, proving, pleasing, and perfecting. I now call these my four P's. These four P's are an infinite loop of the impossible, and it's exhausting. You are never done. You are never enough in this spiraling mindset.

My healing would require breaking free from this mindset and surrendering the fearful habits that resulted. I started to challenge every "What if" and began flipping the fearful worries about the outcomes to ones that were more hopeful, loving, and compassionate. Instead of "What if the chemo does damage to my body?", I considered "What if the chemo is doing exactly what my body needs it to do to combat the cancer cells?" Outside of cancer, there were plenty of examples that fear was running my life. I was working long days and weekends to meet the demands of the four P's. This did not allow for adequate space and time to care for my mind, body, or spirit and was pushing me beyond a healthy, sustainable level.

Have you ever thought to yourself, *What if they don't think that I contributed enough?* Or even more self-critical: *What if I am not enough?* These "contributions" could be in relation to anything—a project at work, a volunteer initiative, social interactions, managing things at home, or parenting children. In these moments, can we find ways to meet our thoughts with love and compassion? Can we flip our thoughts from fear-based to love-based? For example, that may look like, "What if I gave all that I was capable of today?" or "What if I contributed something of value to the collective?" It is a practice of letting go of perfection. It is a practice of letting go of any misconceived ego trip that you are being judged or are the sole contributor. It is a practice of trust!

As we learn, expand our contributions, and heal in life, another powerful shift is letting go of old beliefs and what no longer serves us. Days after my diagnosis, I remember thinking, *What if I don't learn what*

I am meant to learn on this journey? I had more fear around this than the cancer itself.

Prior to cancer, my career focus and passion were helping teams innovate and navigate business problems and opportunities. I loved the "aha moments!" when teams had meaningful conversations, discovered new ideas together, and stretched themselves beyond where they had been, and connecting them to solutions and new opportunities. Cancer empowered me to tap into that experience for myself and create tools and resources I needed to navigate this unpredictable, challenging journey.

The first thing I created was a roadmap of my treatment path and the date this cancer would be "out of me." I needed that visual to focus on when treatments would occur, what came next, and when it would be over. So, while it evolved as I moved through my journey, the "Treatment Roadmap" (as I began to call it) served as the picture telling the larger story that was unfolding in front of me. It later also proved to be effective in sharing updates with family and friends on my CaringBridge site.

I went on to create other tools and resources focused on:

- How to ask for meaningful support
- How to track physical and emotional symptoms in a way that was visually effective for my medical team and me to see patterns and make decisions
- How to capture questions before my appointments and notes in language that I understood (saving hours of calls back to the clinic after the fact)
- How to let go of what wasn't serving me or my health and set new boundaries
- How to identify and create new habits that would support my healing

In the end I had created over thirty tools and resources from diagnosis through my treatments and now in support of my ongoing healing beyond the cancer.

When we surrender old beliefs and fear, we create the space to experiment and open up to new things. We gain freedom from the internal barriers restricting our flow. We can then expand into our full potential. We can transform from the person that we were (in fear) into the person that we were meant to be, centered (in love). Every day is an opportunity to practice, learn, grow, and flow if we come at it with love.

We each contribute something to ourselves, to others, and to the world each and every day. At times we may discount our contributions as insignificant or assume our thoughts and actions have little impact. However, to put this in context, think of how each individual drop of rain plays a role in filling up a bucket. Your daily actions, your decisions, and your mindset all contribute something toward the collective greatness of your life.

Living in an authentic and compassionate way, we can flow with creativity, ideas, and passion. This is the space where we feel strongly that we are in the right place—doing what we are passionate about and making a valuable contribution. I have now taken what used to be meaningful work and shifted to what I believe is my life's work. I could not feel more on purpose. I am on a mission to help others move through their own breast cancer journey with love and an intentional focus on healing the mind, body, and spirit. This set of tools, resources, and an uplifting community are all bundled up and befittingly called "LoveME Healing." I trust that sharing what helped me will help many others with their journeys. I believe our individual greatness contributes to the collective greatness in this world!

There is a gift in today: to challenge your fearful "what ifs," celebrate your wins, meaningfully connect with others AND yourself, as well as to embrace flow and trust your authentic potential.

If you let go of old beliefs that are no longer serving you and turn fear into love, what greatness might lie ahead for you?

LoveMe Healing
Turn Fear Into Love

Maggie Judge
Creator & Founder

Maggie is an energetic, passionate explorer of healing; mind, body and spirit. Her career has been focused on helping teams innovate and navigate business problems with tools and support. Breast Cancer empowered her to tap into that experience and create tools that she needed to help her navigate her unpredictable, challenging journey. She has turned this into her life's work by getting these tools in the hands of others going through breast cancer with LoveME Healing.

maggie@lovemehealing.org
651.235.9361

d in f 🖸 ▶

www.lovemehealing.org

What 'Good to Greatness' Means to Me!
To get to a place where you let go of what doesn't serve you and intentionally create meaningful connection with yourself and others. Trust that when you approach things with Love (vs Fear), you step into your full potential and that is where greatness resides within each of us.

What & Why LoveMe Healing?
LoveME Healing was born out of my personal breast cancer experience and the revelation that my healing meant finding more ways to love and care for myself. My cancer diagnosis was devastating, but the healing journey has been transformational. Our mission is to help others with breast cancer heal; mind, body, and spirit with tools, resources and community.

How to Get Involved:

1) CREATE IMPACT: Champion the movement of 'Healing through Love' by becoming a Gifting Partner. Scan to become a partner.

2) KNOW SOMEONE? Experience a Good to Greatness level of support with the first eBook (of 7), tools and resources in the LoveME Healing Journey. Scan to access free eBook.

Yes, Working Smarter Versus Harder Does Exist

Samantha King, B.Ed.

"Working smarter, not harder" isn't just something people say. I didn't know that at first. When you work in the online business world for as long as I have, you hear all kinds of one-liners that leave you wondering, "What does that even mean?" I know what "Screw the nine-to-five" means, but ask me to definitively tell you what the word *consistency* in "Consistency is key" means, and I don't have a single, one-size-fits-all definition.

I thought "working smarter" meant being more organized to reduce time spent on tasks. And yet, even as I tried to implement that interpretation in my day-to-day operations, I was still working sixty- to eighty-hour weeks. I was no closer to my dream business model—one that I can run from my RV while traveling the world full time with my family. That wasn't going to happen with the business model I had created, and I certainly wasn't going to enjoy it if I had to spend sixty-plus hours a week working just to sustain it. Something had to change.

But honestly, that wasn't the most recent revelation to smack me in the face.

(I will come back to it, though, in a minute.)

The most recent one came to me after the brief bliss of implied vacation that initially accompanied the global shutdown in March 2020. **The realization:** I have no hobbies. Sure, I love to watch TV and had consumed pretty much everything out there by the time the pandemic ended. However, when I was bored, I would go down to my office and work. Don't get me wrong—I love what I do. To a certain extent, my business is my biggest passion, which is good. But I'm not here to be good. I plan on living my greatest life while I'm on this earth, and it trickles into both my personal and professional lives in different ways. The unifying theme, however, is the dream life I want for myself. And it isn't a life where I work up to eighty hours a week or wander down to my office because I'm bored and don't have anything else to be excited about.

I am "Team Anti-Hustle" all the way. I firmly believe that what success looks like for each of us is ours to define. **My Bottom Line:** I didn't leave my teaching job and subsequent corporate jobs to bring home double the workload, all of the meetings, and less of the steady pay. I'm assuming that isn't why you left a job and started this business of yours either.

And yet, many of my course creator clients come to me with the same story. They look around their business one day and realize that rather than the path to freedom and impact that they intended, they've created another job for themselves. And this job has come with less boundaries and more responsibilities than they ever had in corporate. Once upon a time they were nine-to-fivers looking to escape the cubicle and pursue their passions. Yet after their "escape," they still aren't doing that . . . **AND** . . . they've hit an income-earning potential ceiling to boot. They're all out of hours to trade for dollars in the traditional service-based model. I mean, once you've got enough clients to fill your schedule and all your services require you to be on hand to earn money from them, how much higher can you really go? It's tough to continue growing your income if you just keep doing what you've always done. There are only so many hours in the day, after all. But you don't have to continue that way.

As I began to write my chapter for this book, I started by asking myself, "What does Good to Greatness mean to me?" For me, it means leading my course makers community to step into greatness as the subject matter experts they are. Working with them, we co-create a crystal-clear roadmap to efficiently bring their course to the online market platforms and profitably get it into the hands of their ideal audience.

At first, I'll admit, some of them weren't entirely sold on digital courses. They feared adding another thing to their business. How much work would it be? Would it stop people from buying their higher-priced consulting and done-for-you packages? How much of an impact would they really be able to have if they weren't on hand while customers worked through the material? And, finally, that's just not the way it's always been done.

This is what their words were saying, but what I was hearing was "Help! I'm exhausted. I have no more time. I want to do something different, but I can't see the path to the profitable business built to suit my lifestyle that you're talking about, Samantha. I don't know what working smarter and not harder truly means for me." Change is hard. It's hard to leave the comfort of what you've always done. It's hard to see the possibilities when you're in the minutiae of your day-to-day operations.

But what I am asking here is for you to have an open mind and get excited about the potential to break the mold of traditional service businesses. Now, more than ever, is the time to try something innovative. I want you to commit to making a viable plan to move away from only offering consulting, one-on-one sessions, and done-for-you services and move toward adding income streams such as courses into your business model. What I see for you, if you do this, is economic innovation for yourself. A place in your life where you are "working smarter, not harder" to create your own economy of additional income streams that work together to help more people and increase your impact tenfold.

Do digital courses make money? This is a fair question. We're talking about adding an income stream to your business, aren't we? **Let me say this:** During the pandemic, the digital course industry was booming. Its projected worth as an industry increased by $73 billion dollars. We are anticipating a net industry worth of almost $400 billion by the year 2026. Those numbers aren't bad.

An equally important stat to consider? Student demand stats. The good news is that student demand is on the rise, and the biggest increases are not in the industries you think. Business and Marketing saw an increase in student demand of 1820 percent, but that number was even bigger for niches like Arts and Entertainment (2,500 percent) and Fashion and

Beauty (2,300 percent). What that tells us is that courses paid off big for businesses who would never traditionally consider this income stream. Their willingness to innovate during a time where they couldn't continue offering their services in ways they traditionally had (*I'm looking at you, global rolling shutdowns*) paid off in a big way. Furthermore, it allowed them to control their economic results during a time of unprecedented uncertainty for this generation.

With Zoom calls quickly becoming the norm, makeup artists, personal stylists, and jewelers were creating courses that taught people how to make that on-screen real estate look its best. Home decor pros, interior designers, and lighting companies were out there teaching those same Zoom-goers how to set up the area behind them to look professional. We saw home organizers teaching people how to declutter their houses as we were faced with the messes around the house that we had been ignoring. Landscapers and gardeners joined in on the movement when spring hit to help us revolutionize the backyards where we would unexpectedly be spending our summer.

Possibility and economic innovations were everywhere. Hobby-based courses began to trend as people spent their time rediscovering passions and finding new ones. I read a case study from Shopify where one of their customers—a bike parts shop—saw a revitalization in interest for cycling (*it really is the perfect social-distancing sport*) so they created courses filled with how-tos that featured their products throughout. Course buyers were clamoring to spend their money on the products they had seen in action and wanted to spend those dollars with the bike store that had got them excited to start cycling again.

During the last two cohorts of my Monetize My Course program, I worked with a YouTuber for quilters who was creating a collection of courses and a writer creating a course about how to write your own fan-fiction. I have worked with event planners, mental health professionals, and nonprofit sponsorship experts to add a digital course income stream to their business. Right now, so many of us are looking to take our financial situation into our own hands. For me, digital courses were the first step to truly understand what "working smarter, not harder" meant for me. And for my clients, digital courses have been the residual revenue stream that has allowed them to bring in increased income **AND** create that time freedom in their business to pursue the passions they left corporate to pursue.

SAMANTHA KING
Course Developer / Strategist

When teaching in the classroom wasn't the right fit anymore, Samantha carved out her own path. As a course creator, she quickly become frustrated with an industry that teaches others to create courses their buyers won't finish and is reluctant to share the roadmap to course sales success. Now Samantha demystifies course creation and selling for her community. She has helped countless subject matter experts profitably teach what they know to the next generation!

samantha@sellyouronlinecourse.com

WHAT 'GOOD TO GREATNESS' MEANS TO ME!

For me, it means leading my course makers community to st into greatness as the subject matter experts they are. Worki with them, we co-create a crystal-clear roadmap to efficient bring their course to the online market platforms and profita get it into the hands of their ideal audience.

MONETIZE MY COURSE PROGRAM

A simple, methodical method to map out and revenue-gener your digital course(s).

Includes:
- 7-weeks live training sessions with Samantha (recorc
- Personalized, instruction every session; meet you wh you're at!
- 1:1 x 30-minute brainstorm session to establish your goals
- Workbook, planner, templates every time you create new course
- Weekly online office hours for solutions between sessions
- Session recordings for 60-days post program conclus
- BONUS
  ○ 45-day access to The Course Creators Den A membership hub to successfully integrate you course(s) into your business model. Connect wit other course creators for ideas, collaboration an sales tips

Book a 30-minute Free Brainstorm!
Scan QR code to book!

samantha KING
Creating & Marketing Your Top Selling Course Just Got Easier

in f ⓟ

www.heysamanthaking.com

Infinite Creativity, Resilience, and Love

Lesia Daria Kohut

Initially, when I was asked to participate in the *Good to Greatness* campaign, my response was, "Thank you, but not at this time."

I was in the final five months of ministerial studies, I had just published my first book, *Soul Excavation: An Exploration and Discovery of Self Through Fear, Failure, and Quantum Physics*, and was busy promoting it, and I was working part time while building my spiritual coaching business. Thanks to my new book, I had speaking engagements booked through the next three months. Thanks to focusing on my business, I was steadily attracting more ideal clients.

I was also, however, grieving the sudden loss of a dear friend, and, thanks to accidentally smashing my face with the liftgate of our car, was navigating the symptoms of a concussion. For weeks, I felt "off," unable to access words and names of people I knew. I'd be in conversation with someone or giving a talk when, suddenly, my brain would shut off. One moment I'd be speaking, and the next it was as if I'd quantum leapt into a reality where I had no idea what had just happened or what I was talking about. I knew these blips would eventually pass. However, the confusion, impatience, and even embarrassment I felt because of not being able to think, speak, and act with my usual curiosity, clarity, and enthusiasm left me feeling frustrated and, more often than not, exhausted.

The very thought of taking on this project, especially with the tight deadline of only three to four weeks, was enough to make my already-spinning head whirl right off its axis.

And yet, during a lively, engaging, and thought-provoking Monday Mindset call with members of the Reset Collective (an online networking and collaboration group), I began to feel differently.

I had just shared a story with the group about saying yes to an opportunity from the previous year. At the time, even though I had no idea how I was going to pay for the intensive six-month program I'd just signed up for or how I'd be able to fit the work involved into my already super-full schedule, I allowed myself to make this exciting, nerve-wracking, and slightly terrifying decision from my vision rather than where I was in that moment. Why? Because I knew if I didn't say yes, there was no way anything was going to change.

As the Monday Mindset conversation continued, I could feel the same enthusiasm and excitement I'd felt a year earlier begin to bubble up. Even with everything I was already committed to, the ear-to-ear grin on my face, tingling in my body, quickening of my heartbeat, and butterflies in my stomach indicated that I was already leaning in. Instantaneously, I fast-forwarded to the future and considered: *If I were to look back at this moment one, two, or five years from now, what decision would I have made today that would allow me to later say, "I'm so grateful and thankful I made that choice?"* In that moment, I knew and felt that the only possible answer was yes.

In the four decades before setting foot on my spiritual path, however, I wasn't even aware of most of the choices I was making. I believed the world was a dualistic one where there were good people and bad people, positive and negative experiences, that you were either a success or a failure and life was either worth living or it wasn't. When it came to making a decision, I'd be so afraid of the consequences of making the wrong one (as my all-too-familiar loop of "You're not good enough," "You're not smart enough," and "You don't have what it takes" played repeatedly in my mind), oftentimes, I wouldn't make a decision at all. The result? I stayed stuck in a self-fulfilling prophecy of limitation grounded in pain, anger, and fear.

Although I had spent a couple of decades working with various counselors and therapists to process the traumas of my childhood and early adulthood, it wasn't until I began the spiritual leg of my journey of self-discovery that I came to realize what a limited, victim-oriented existence I'd been living.

The very first thing I learned in spiritual/consciousness studies was that what I think and how I use my mind are directly related to how I experience my life. By changing my thinking, I could literally change my life.

How liberating it was to discover that I wasn't as powerless as I'd felt, that life wasn't as fatalistic as I'd thought it to be! How monumental to discover that there was no great entity pulling any proverbial puppet strings—that I, and no one else, was in control of my life experience.

What I also learned is that what we focus on expands. The more we place our attention on something, the more what we're focusing on will become our life experience. So, when we focus on—knowingly or unknowingly—"You're not good enough, "You're not smart enough," or "You don't have what it takes," guess what? We'll continue to attract the opportunities and create experiences to support those very hypotheses. The only way we can break the cycle of those limiting beliefs is to consciously choose to do so.

Now, there are also moments that the pull, the beckoning, even the siren call to greatness, is so powerful and compelling that it, too, cannot be ignored. If you've ever experienced a calling, you know what I'm talking about.

Unlike the siren song in Greek mythology that would literally direct sailors to their doom, however, a true calling is one that comes from within the very depths of our soul, impelling and activating us into living our life's purpose. This is the calling of our greatness. And when greatness comes calling, the only response that will allow us to experience the greatness rushing its way to the surface is yes.

For me, the call to ministry has been the most delineating invitation to greatness so far. In one life-altering moment, I felt my entire body come alive with meaning, value, potentiality, and a willingness to say yes. I heard and felt in every single cell, system, and organ that my purpose in this life was profound yet simple and unequivocal: to love. The best way I could embrace, embody, and cultivate love was to become a minister.

I'm now three months away from officially becoming a minister of New Thought. During the past seven years, I've had numerous opportunities to further immerse myself in and embody the concepts of oneness, wholeness, interconnectivity. More importantly, my journey of ministry has opened me up to the realization and responsibility of walking the talk in every aspect of my life, every moment of every day, of never stepping off principle, of always being in integrity—*in wholeness*—with and as the Infinite Creativity, Resilience, and Love—the greatness—I now know myself to be.

That being said, there is one New Thought meme that tends to get my back up: We are spiritual beings having a human experience. I'd like to challenge that notion by declaring that we are spiritual beings having a *spiritual* experience. That we, as pure Energy/Spirit/Love, are all unique, original expressions of Infinite Creativity, Resilience, and Love—enjoying and fulfilling itself in, through, and as us.

There are plenty of reminders to keep us focused on our limitations. If we really want to live our greatness, it's time for us to consciously focus on the infinite potentiality of who and what we truly are rather than simply accept the finite humanness that is merely an aspect of our beingness.

When I make a decision from my vision instead of from where I am today, I am consciously choosing to let go of the old thoughts, stories, and beliefs that have gotten me to this moment and open up to something new. I am trusting and knowing that—no matter how unnerving or terrifying it might feel to say yes—I am fully supported every step of the way, now and always.

Living our greatness is about being willing to continually step out of our comfort zone. It's about leaning into, embracing, and embodying the infinite Energy/Spirit/Love we truly are. It's about consciously choosing to know that we are spiritual beings having a *spiritual* experience. It's about being in integrity—in every aspect of our life—even when it's hard, and especially when no one's watching. It's about making decisions from our vision to challenge, stretch, and propel ourselves into possibilities we couldn't have imagined, trusting and knowing that—no matter what—

all the resources required to make our decision right are available to us right here, right now, and always.

So, my question to you is: *Are you ready and willing to live your greatness?* The choice is yours.

You are Infinite Creativity, Resilience, and Love. Now act like it.

Lesia Kohut AcsB, RScP, INHC
Infinite Creativity, Resilience, and Love

Lesia Daria Kohut
Soul Excavator

A self-professed Soul Excavator, Lesia looks for the beauty, harmony, and love in everyone and everything. A speaker, author, podcaster, and coach, Lesia enjoys living in the question; seeing every moment as a brand-new opportunity to heal, grow, and expand; and revels in embracing the mysticism of spirituality and infinite possibilities of the quantum realm to further empower the conscious awakening of humanity so that together we can cultivate a global community founded in Love.

lesia@lesiakohut.com
250.208.0968

What 'Good to Greatness' Means to Me!

Living our greatness is being willing to continually step out of our comfort zone and intentionally live as Infinite Creativity, Resilience, and Love. This includes making decisions from our vision, living in integrity, and always focusing on the infinite Energy/Spirit/Love we truly are rather than arguing for our limitations.

Soul Excavation

(n.)/ The mindful, messy, and dynamic work of digging through and unearthing the limiting thoughts, stories, and beliefs that keep us feeling stuck; revealing Life's most extraordinary treasure—the Infinite Creativity, Resilience, and Love we truly are!

Soul Excavation: An Exploration of Self Through Fear, Failure, and Quantum Physics is about one woman's transformational journey of living from pain, anger, and fear to discovering and choosing to live as the Infinite Power, Creativity, and Love she is at her core.

Bravely, candidly, and vulnerably, Lesia Kohut shares three personal stories and accompanying vignettes to illustrate her transformation from fear and failure to infinite possibilities, showing us that just because life has been a certain way up until now, doesn't mean it has to be that way going forward.

Lesia Daria Kohut

Soul
Excavation

An Exploration and Discovery of Self Through
Fear, Failure, and Quantum Physics

Purchase your copy today on:
Amazon
Barnes & Noble
Chapters / Indigo
and wherever e-Books are sold

f ▶ **in** ⊙

www.lesiakohut.com

Consciously Creating and Upleveling Your Love Story

Heather Leah

What does it mean to go from good to greatness in *your love story*?

What would an experience of "Greatness" look like for you in *your love story*?

In my love story, I have experienced going from "Good to Greatness" every time I look at my own automatic relationship thinking, examine it, and then release old thinking or beliefs that no longer serve me or the love relationship.

I have noticed that once I release my robotic or automatic beliefs, my relationship capacity expands, allowing me to generate greater expression of authentic love for myself and my partner.

There are several obvious areas of life where assumed love and relationship beliefs or automatic thinking can creep into our lives. If left unexamined, they can unintentionally run our love bus and relationship choices without us even being aware.

The most visible love and relationship influencers and influences in our lives are:

- Significant family members
- Societal norms
- Religion
- Cultural heritage
- Media, including romance novels, television, and movies

When I developed my *Love Relationship Blueprint*, I was able to see ways in which my love relationship thinking was shaped by the actions and behaviors of significant family members. A very prominent area of my love relationship behavior was shaped by my mother.

The uncertainty and volatility of my mom's childhood shaped her strong sense of responsibility as she assumed the traditional female role of caretaker for her mother, brother, and subsequently her four children and my father. At times I have watched her inadvertently become overly responsible, taking ownership of family members chores, problems, or emotions.

You've heard the saying, "The apple doesn't fall far from the tree," right? Well, "like mother, like daughter," I too have had to grapple with my own sense of over-responsibility for partners, parents, or family members. For example, the times I pay more attention to the needs of others than I do my own or do things just because they need to get done and then feel resentful after I have completed them or get annoyed at the apparent "irresponsibility" of others.

One of the men in my *Love Relationship Blueprint* who caused my soul to grow and expand significantly was Mr. Childlike.[1] When I examined my thinking, I could see that I was thinking that "someone has to do it," which played right into my habit of being overly responsible.

I put more time, energy, and money into generating a relationship that was draining and depleting me. Each time I focused on the household chores, paying the bills, taking care of the pets, or dealing with his personal needs instead of my own, I could see that I was participating in the relationship more like a parent than a partner.

This time frame was a turning point in our relationship. I recently had learned about a very gifted clairvoyant in San Francisco, and one of his services was soul journey readings. I scheduled an appointment with him to see if I could gain more insight into what else I needed to learn.

The day came for my soul reading. I had never met this man or talked with him before. He asked me for my full name and birthdate. He was still for several moments and then noted that he was going to walk me

---

[1] *IS HE MR. RIGHT...OR MR. RIGHT NOW?*, by Heather Leah, Chapter 7, "Semiconscious Stepping Over Signs."

through where I was on my soul's journey. He began with the following story:

It is snowing heavily outside and bitterly cold. You are downtown, standing on one of the four corners of a moderately busy street. Across the street, a bus arrives. It stops at the bus stop, and opens its doors, allowing passengers to disembark or climb aboard. You see an elderly woman slowly get off the bus, managing each step to ensure she does not fall. She begins to put on her gloves and drops one of them in the snow.

Then he stopped the story and asked me, "What do you want to do?"

I replied, "Run across the street and help her."

He noted that he wanted me to stay on my side of the street and continue to watch. Then he continued.

The elderly woman bends over to get the glove, and instead of pulling it out of the snow, she buries it further below, making it harder to retrieve. She rubs her one glove and exposed hand together trying keep her shaking hands warm. She is teetering a bit as she struggles to balance, bending over to dig deeper in the piling snow.

Again, he stopped the story and asked me, "What do you want to do?"

I replied, "Run across the street, dig out her glove, and help her." He noted that he wanted me to continue to hold myself back from "helping."

Even though I know he is telling me a story, I am literally experiencing my anguish and angst over this hypothetical elderly woman whom I can't rescue.

The elderly woman shifts her body, getting as close to the snow-covered ground as she can, so she can dig her glove out. She looks around to see if someone is coming her way. She keeps shivering as the wind blows more snow on top of her buried glove.

The clairvoyant asked me, "What do you want to do?" At this point in time, it is all I can do to keep myself from bolting across the street to take care of the old woman. I told him exactly how I was feeling inside. He noted that he wanted me to continue to stay on my side of the street and hold myself back from "helping." Then he urged me to keep watching.

The elderly woman painfully rooted around in the snow and was still unable to recover the second glove. She finally gave up her struggle and turned to walk back to the corner. She crossed the street and went into a store, where for months she had long been eyeing a pair of leather cashmere-lined gloves. She emerged from the store beaming and satisfied that she had finally made this purchase for herself. As she walked away, she disposed of her remaining old glove in the trash bin just outside of the building, happily walking to her destination now with her warm hands wrapped in beautiful gloves.

A homeless woman, sitting inside a building entryway on the other corner of the street had been watching the unfolding scene intensely. She appeared seemingly out of nowhere, plucked one glove out of the trash can, then crossed the street and dug the other glove out of the snow. She placed both gloves on her hands and she was grateful for the new gloves to keep her warm.

The clairvoyant gently pointed out that I, *in my spiritual arrogance,* think that I know better what other people need, that I know what's better for them, when I rush in to "help" or do things for them that they are completely capable of doing for themselves.

He was undeniably right, and every cell in my body knew it. I had just listened to a story—a story, mind you—and it fatigued me to stop myself emotionally and physically from going across the street to help the elderly woman. My mind began to race back over my relationships with family, friends, and men from my past. Where had I been a disabling friend, family member, or romantic partner by not staying on my side of the street, by parenting instead of partnering?

It was extremely clear that had I stepped in and "helped" that elderly woman, she would not have experienced the joy and richness of owning a pair of cashmere-lined leather gloves, and the homeless woman would not have known the warmth of those gloves left behind that she was able to retrieve. Where else might I have prohibited someone else's full experience or soul expansion because I was "caretaking," being overly responsible, or had stepped in uninvited?

By examining my assumed behaviors from family influencers and automatic thinking from societal norms, I was free to begin letting go of my over-responsibility habit in favor of finding a more appropriate balance. It was clear to me that staying on my side of the relationship street would reduce the burden on my shoulders, create more space for my partner to contribute, and allow me to refocus my energy on developing my abilities making specific, well-defined requests in areas where I desired additional support from my partner.

If you desire to have your love relationships go from good to greatness, whether they are family, friend, or romantic love partnerships, examining your automatic thinking and beliefs just might reveal nuggets of liberating gold for you!

Introspection Questions

1. Are there areas in your life where you experience carrying more than your fair share of responsibility?
2. Whose needs and wants do you pay more attention to while ignoring your own?
3. Where do you secretly feel resentful of your partner, friends, or family members?
4. Where might your over responsibility be disempowering others or reducing their self-confidence in their own abilities?

Heather Leah, LLC

Consciously Create Your Luscious Love Story

Heather Leah
Conscious Creator

Heather Leah is passionate about shining a light on outdated relationship thinking and limiting beliefs so we can co-create a world where every woman has a voice and a choice - because there is nothing more attractive than a woman in love with her own life! Heather Leah brings her leadership skills in organizational change, personal growth, and executive coaching to her work with women around the world.

heather@consciouslycreateyourlovestory.com
202-642-0983

What 'Good to Greatness' Means to Me!

The great relationship I enjoy now is constantly expanding, evolving, and deepening us as individuals and our flourishing partnership. My previous relationships ranged from depleting to delightful but never reached the level of great until I stopped settling for good enough. When you release beliefs that no long serve you, you can consciously create your GREAT love story

Love Relationship Blueprint Program

A creative and profoundly impactful 4 step process that will up-level your ability to attract your heart's desire.

Your powerful outcomes:

- Identify influences that have dominated your relationship results and make new liberating choices
- Reframe the unconscious habits that have blocked t relationships you long for
- Become irresistible - acknowledge the best in yourse and create your sacred self-love program
- Consciously create your relationship blueprint for designing your luscious love story

Don't Spend Another Day Longing For Love!
Register Now: $297

SCAN QR CODE TO REGISTER

consciouslycreateyourlovestory.com

In the Present Moment

Sam Liebowitz

The gift of being present is one of the greatest gifts we can give ourselves and others. My own life, while challenging at times, has shown me the importance of fully living with our awareness focused on what is happening right here, right now. Over the years, I've come to know both the difficulties as well as the benefits of such a practice, as well as experiencing the freedom that can come from it.

I never realized how much I tried to be not present to my life. From the time I was a child, living with parents who were emotionally unavailable because of their own challenges, I just wanted to be somewhere else. I remember how the red-brick house I grew up in always felt cold. Not just physically cold, but emotionally cold. I couldn't articulate that at the time; I could only feel it.

My parents were not bad people. They were never abusive, and they truly did the best they could. They were just human beings who were of a generation that didn't know how to deal with trauma. Still, I can vividly remember not wanting to be a part of my family because I never felt connected to my parents or my siblings the way I other kids seemed to be. I never felt like I belonged. I just wanted to disappear from this world.

That might be why I got into drugs when I was in high school. With marijuana, LSD, mescaline, and other psychedelics, I could escape those feelings. Like everyone else my age, I engaged with these substances recreationally, with no guidance and no real idea of what I was doing. I was lucky that I was never drawn to truly addictive things like cocaine or narcotics.

The other thing I found by using drugs was community. For the first time, I found people who didn't bully or make fun of me. The other kids who were also doing drugs accepted me as I was. That was a new experience for me.

When I went to college, I moved away from doing so many drugs, although I still smoked pot once in a while. I started to be a little more present to my life, and that brought a lot of up-and-down feelings.

It was there that I became good friends with a guy named Alex; he was very peculiar and smart. He and others introduced me to the world of spirituality.

As I got to know Alex, I was drawn into his world. He would tell me about his ideas for science, fiction stories until the early hours of the morning. Alex experienced unusual coincidences that brought him to his spiritual path. Books about mysticism, gnosticism, and other spiritual topics would fall off shelves in front of him at the bookstore.

In time, it became clear Alex had mental health problems. One day when he was reading his girlfriend Rosemarie's psychology textbook, he found that he had all the classic signs of schizophrenia. He knew this was a problem, but he refused to go see a psychiatrist or psychologist. After a several months, when his student loan money started to run out, I stepped up and told him I would help support him until he could get past the illness and was able to work.

However, things got worse. Rosemarie moved in with him and dropped out of school to help him as the frequency of the psychotic breaks increased, and so did the money trouble.

Even though I was still in school and working parttime, I ended up supporting both of them. Rosemarie would try to get what jobs she could, but as Alex's condition got more unstable, she would miss work, get fired, or just quit. I started working fulltime and going to school parttime in order to make enough money to support them. I eventually graduated, but it became a living hell to come home each night to find Alex freaking out and doing things like hitting himself or breaking his glasses or other things in the apartment. Once again, I did my best to escape the present moment because it was so hard to deal with what was happening in front of my eyes. I took a second evening job so that I would have to leave early in the morning and not come back until after 9:00 p.m. at night.

After six years of this, I knew I had to get out. The owners sold the building where we were renting, so we had to move. I helped Alex and Rosemarie find another place but did not move with them. I asked my mom if I could move back in with her, and to my amazement, she agreed.

I still supported Alex and Rosemarie for a few years after that, but eventually I told them I couldn't give them any more money. After that, I never heard from them again. I was finally free from the nightmare, yet I was still riddled with guilt and shame over leaving them without any support.

It took a long time to heal from that experience. In fact, I am probably still healing from it. In time, I got married to a wonderful woman, a therapist, and I began my healing journey in earnest.

First, I got back into some personal development courses. I discovered various healing modalities, and I started taking classes on everything from the Sedona Method to Reiki. Not that I ever thought I would become a healer; it was all for my own healing. Yet the universe had other plans for me, and I did eventually become a healer.

After studying with various spiritual teachers and groups for several years, I finally decided to find my own path. I didn't know what that meant; I just knew it was time for me to move on.

Less than a year later, in May 2014, my life took a dramatic change. My wife had gone to a psychology conference in China, so I was alone for the first weekend in years. That Friday afternoon, I got a text from a friend about an open house at someone's apartment seven blocks from my apartment. I had nothing else to do, so I went.

When I got to the place and my friend arrived, I asked him what it was all about. He told me they did plant medicine ceremonies together and I should come to one they were having the next day in Brooklyn. Initially, I told him I wasn't interested. Many of the spiritual teachers and groups I had been with had been very negative about the idea of using substances for spiritual growth.

Yet as I was walking back to my apartment that night, I thought to myself, *This is the only weekend in the entire year that I'm free and have space to say yes. I can try it once, and if I don't like it, I never have to see any of these people again.* I called my friend the next morning and told him I would go.

That one decision changed my life. During that ceremony, I had a huge energetic release. Even though I had done a lot of healing work around the experiences in my life, it was nothing like this ceremony. I felt as if I had dropped a thousand-pound weight off my shoulders that I didn't even know was there. For the first time in my life, I became present to how much pain and sadness I had been carrying for years.

I have continued to do this deep inner ceremonial work. I have not only released years of anguish I had been holding on to, but I have also healed my relationships with my parents, my family, and most of all, myself. I have learned to forgive myself for the many decisions I made in the past. The truly amazing thing is that as I healed and released my own trauma, I have become more able to be in the present moment. I can now be present to and hold space for challenging situations that come up. I am kinder to myself and others. I am less angry and more able to truly share space and hold space for another human being.

When we are able to truly feel things we have held on to our whole life, to let the pain flow through us and not latch on to it, those things no longer take us out of presence. By integrating the transcendent experiences of medicine work into my daily life, I have learned to see life's perfection and be less judgmental of all that's happened to me. The true gift of this work has been the ability to appreciate and truly be present to each and every moment of my life.

All of life is lived in the present moment. Ultimately, that is all we really have. Let's not waste our time on this earth running away from what is happening to us. To learn to live in this present moment is the greatest gift we can give ourselves!

THE CONSCIOUS CONSULTANT

You are more powerful than you know!

SAM LIEBOWITZ
The Conscious Consultant

Sam Liebowitz, known as The Conscious Consultant, is a facilitator, mentor, speaker, healer, serial entrepreneur, host of the top rated radio show, The Conscious Consultant Hour, and is a two time best-selling author, and author of the #1 empowerment book, Everyday Awakening.

He has been in business since 1993 and has owned several successful businesses. His current ventures include TALKRADIO.NYC, and Double Diamond Wellness in Manhattan. Sam has lectured in several venues, including being a featured speaker at TEDxUpperWestSide in 2016.

sam@theconsciousconsultant.com
212.721.8183

WHAT 'GOOD TO GREATNESS' MEANS TO ME!

To truly be great in this life, it is all about being present to the journey we are on. To show up with an open heart and mind, and be ready to face whatever life brings your way with humility, integrity, and honesty.

THE INTEGRATION PROGRAM

You have had a psychedelic experience in the last 6 -12 months. My program helps you integrate it.

- 6-week online integration sessions whether at home or abroad
- Utilize the amazing experience in your daily life
- Integrate the shifts, healing and awareness for long-term positive change
- Live the changes you've desired for your life

Ready for your free Integration checkup?
Scan QR code to book!

in f ⊙ ▶ y

www.theconsciousconsultant.com

Hello Growth, Goodbye Comfort Zone!

Rie Lowe

I once read a quote: "There's no growth in the comfort zone, and no comfort in the growth zone." This is what propelled me from Good to Greatness.

When I was growing up, I didn't know anything about greatness. In fact, I barely knew anything about good. In my family, things were hard for me. I was raised in a broken home—a single parent household in the late 1970s, a time when divorce wasn't very common. I had a big brother who hated me and wasn't afraid to show it. We were poor, so that meant wearing my brother's hand-me-down clothes instead of the cute styles other girls were into. My mom, as much as she loved me, made me feel less valued than my brother because I was a girl. My family adhered to some pretty traditional gender roles because . . . well, that's just how it was. I was raised believing that girls grow up to become wives and mothers. If you wanted to work, it was pretty simple. You had three choices: nurse, secretary, or teacher. Not that there was anything wrong with any of those life paths—it's just that I didn't understand why things had to be so limited simply because I wasn't male. Even with all that, I believed that there was something better out there for me. I decided not to be bound by restrictive thoughts, especially those projected upon me by other people.

Limiting beliefs were never my thing. When I was told I couldn't do something, you'd better believe that I was going to do it. I guess this is what led me to embrace my inner rebel as a moody, fourteen-year-old teenager, much to the dismay of my worried mother. The more rules I had thrown at me, the more rules I broke. After quite a few bumps in the road, I finally learned to harness that adolescent, rule-breaking rebel attitude and wield it in a constructive instead of destructive way.

Rather than trying to break rules, as an adult, I wanted to break the glass ceiling. Although I didn't know it, what I was rebelling against as a teen were the limitations put on me simply because I was female. Now, as a full-fledged adult in the working world, I was quick to realize that it wasn't just my family dynamic that saw me as "less than" based on gender—it was the corporate structure as well.

Due to this, I aimed to overachieve in any position I held, speak up and out during meetings, and advocate for what was right in my workplace. What I found over and over again, was that my behavior seemed to put a target on my back. Instead of experiencing support and appreciation as I was expecting, I endured gaslighting and bullying—oddly enough, more from women than men. I encountered many women who were saddled with limited beliefs about competition in the workplace. As much as I would have liked to change the world, it was much more practical for me to change my personal path. It was time for a bold move. *Hello growth!*

Since realizing that scaling the corporate ladder wasn't as feasible as I had hoped, I decided to create my own ladder—and jump straight to the top! I made the risky move of becoming an entrepreneur and creating one of Canada's first social media marketing agencies in 2013.

In this new and emerging industry, my little start-up quickly grew and became the go-to resource for businesses wanting to get ahead of their competition online. My company successfully handled the accounts of numerous happy clients. I had to secure more office space and hire teams of people. Sales offices hired me to train their agents on building their brand and clientele online. I received continuous requests to deliver workshops for both new entrepreneurs starting out with social media and experienced business owners wanting to learn advanced techniques. Over the next eight years, my company won dozens of awards in multiple locations. In fact, I was honored as Entrepreneur of the Year in 2019! As my reputation grew, so did the invitations I received to speak about social media marketing at groups, events, and conferences locally, nationally, and even globally.

Timing played an important role in my company's success, being at the forefront of an emerging industry. Another key element was that I was able to make the most of my connecting and relationship-building skills. Since my two offices were located in smaller communities, away from the big city, we had the reputation of being the friendly, local business you could trust. My team and I certainly personified that image and used it to build the brand. Business was good, and even though we had some great momentum, success, and brand credibility, being located outside of major hubs also brought its share of challenges.

What had propelled us to a great level of success suddenly became an obstacle as countless competitors popped up each year, especially those located in major cities. Instead of building on our solid reputation, we were now tasked with defending it. The big-city businesses felt that a marketing firm from our area code couldn't meet their standards and expectations. This, of course, was a false, limiting belief. Our team was highly experienced and continuously increasing their skills. Nevertheless, this challenge presented itself time and time again.

Our mandate had always been to support and empower local businesses, so we tried to keep our focus there. As the industry evolved, our services had to evolve as well. This brought upon another obstacle. Many of the small businesses that could really use our help were more traditional in their thoughts about marketing. Online methods didn't always resonate with them, so an ongoing investment wasn't of interest to them. For those who clearly understood the importance and value of having a digital marketing strategy, it was a no-brainer to reach out to us for help, but they often had unrealistic expectations with extremely limited budgets. Finding a good balance between being profitable yet affordable as well as being able to achieve concrete results for our clients was a never-ending challenge. It was time for a different approach.

Obstacles are inevitable in business, but when we break through our limiting beliefs about them, they become opportunities for even greater success. Again, it was time for a bold move, but this one was a true leap of faith. *Goodbye comfort zone!*

Although my business was continuing to grow, something in me felt stagnant. Perhaps it was that I had achieved the goals I had originally set for myself when I started my business. It could have been an age thing, or maybe an empty-nest issue. Whatever the driving force was, I knew I needed change. I was stuck in the comfort zone, and it was time to break free.

When I started my business, I created, posted, and managed content for my client's social media platforms. As I evolved in my business, I truly fell in love with the teaching aspect: speaking, training, consulting, and conducting workshops. I didn't get to do enough of it; my business model wasn't set up to support those revenue streams properly. If I wanted to excel in an area of business that brought me authentic joy, I needed to shake things up—a lot.

In 2019, I decided to leave everything behind and focus on going from good to greatness. I left my creative director in charge of overseeing my two offices in Ontario. I packed up my belongings, said goodbye to my loved ones, took one last look at the life I had known for so long, and drove across the country.

Four days later, I landed in beautiful Vancouver, a city where I knew virtually no one—a city that didn't know me. I couldn't ride on my past success; instead, I had to start from scratch. I needed to tap into those connecting and relationship-building skills. I had to channel my inner rebel, the one who was never one to fail. I would have to build an entirely new business . . . on my own. Scary? Yes. But growth doesn't happen in the comfort zone.

Now, three years (and one pandemic) later, I've started a second business and sold my previous one in order to focus my services in a way that brings me happiness and satisfaction. I'm fortunate to be invited to speak at groups, events, and conferences. I provide valuable services that help other entrepreneurs find the level of success they envision.

Limited beliefs would have me define success by a bank account. I'm no Jeff Bezos, so I might be considered a failure in that department. But I know that if we change our mindset, we change our results. I'm able to focus on doing what I love. I'm manifesting my own destiny. I'm living authentically. I've taken my business from good to greatness!

Rie Lowe
Owner

Rie Lowe is a Social Media & Digital Marketing Motivator, Strategist and International Speaker with over 25 years of experience. She is an award-winning entrepreneur who educates, inspires and encourages personal brands, business owners, sales professionals and service providers to grow their clientele. As a motivational speaker, Rie has spoken to audiences worldwide and has been cited as being a top authority on building your brand online by connecting with your target audience.

rie@rielowe.com
504-789-8281

What 'Good to Greatness' Means to Me!

I love helping businesses go from Good to Greatness. They come with a *good* idea that they need digital marketing to grow and they end up with a *great* strategy, training and support. My secret to success is a combination of vision, attitude and adaptability. See it, believe it, be it.

"Reach New Heights" Strategic Plan

A customized strategy helps create maximum impact in your digital marketing efforts.

Includes:
- Analysis of current online presence
- Full discovery call
- Brand and target market identification
- Strategy report: website, blog, newsletter, social media and more
- Content and hashtag recommendations
- Follow up call

Scan Here for a Complimentary 30-min Mini Analysis & Ask the Expert

digital marketing

in f ⓞ ♪ 🐦

www.rielowe.com

Journey from Separate to Whole

Whitney Merritt

From symptoms to system
From mind-body to vital force
From human to non-human-specific
From confusion to clarity
From arbitration to specific method
To increasing levels of success . . .
May we reach the depth
That spirit can rise!

—Rajan Sankaran

For my spirit to rise, I journeyed from separate to whole, from hidden to healed and actualized my innate being. As a young child, I sensed myself as a spirit being. I wondered at creation and felt a deep and profound connection with nature and people. I moved with the trees blowing in the wind and merged with the waters. I flew in my dreams and in my mind's eye. I felt the richness of our souls. My heart sang with the smile of another, a kind look, a warm embrace, and I sensed the Oneness uniting us all. My journey from good to greatness came as this inner knowing actualized. Seeming separation brought me home to the ALL as *I became me within the ONE.*

I came to understand the nature of my soul, the process of birth and death, and the nature of vibrational healing. My journey has been to remember who I am, to see where we all fit together, and to activate each of our Divine blueprints to awaken our innate self as Source. Imagine understanding and operating with your body, mind, and soul in alignment. How can we create, live fully, and be masters in our own life if we do not know how we are wired and designed? Let's explore some of this together.

My professional experience includes THE CHART, BRIDGE, NAET (Nambudripad's Allergy Elimination Technique), and Homeopathy. THE CHART gives an overarching understanding of your soul and personality. BRIDGE and NAET operate on the foundations of Traditional Chinese Medicine. Homeopathy elegantly provides understanding of the nature of the spirit and vibrational medicine. Intuitively I was shown how to blend the ancient arts together, and my clientele began to swiftly heal.

Your Soul and Personality

Our souls made contracts and agreements before we landed in bodies. We chose specific body types, families, friends, societies, and frameworks to complete our karma and evolve. Sometimes our soul self even chose a specific goal in this lifetime to learn and master. We each have a unique signature, personality structure, and a way that we are energetically wired. Imagine the life expansion with this knowledge!

THE CHART

THE CHART is a tool I utilize that has helped me immeasurably in my life and in the lives of my clients and friends. This powerful tool is a tangible, practical, and applicable framework that can be applied every second you live. It illustrates your soul age, your goal (how your soul chooses to evolve), your attitude (how you see the world), your chief features (accelerate or block growth), your mode (the way you are energetically wired), and even your body type. There are seven possible combinations in each category, and we also have access to the entire chart consisting of forty-nine aspects. THE CHART demonstrates what alignment feels like when we are in our positive poles and what misalignment feels like when we are in our negative poles. It shows us how to operate from higher or lower consciousness. When we are triggered emotionally, we can see which negative pole is active and promptly find the action to move us out of the painful moment. For example, if someone has a goal of GROWTH in their chart, the negative pole is -*confusion*. The action to take is a move toward +*simplicity*, which activates the positive pole +*evolution*. There is no judgement, but rather a map to help us rise above our negative poles.

Imagine you are an OLD soul born to BABY soul parents. BABY souls learn through *black-and-white thinking* and do not see the magnificent colors in the world. There is nothing wrong with either perspective; it is simply what their soul is actualizing. OLD souls learn through *oneness* and, in the realm of time, have a deeper understanding and a real lived experience of simply knowing things. When this is understood, an OLD soul can shift their expectations of a BABY soul parent. There is a soul recognition and resonance with this information. As this happens, we learn to operate from our positive poles more frequently, and we can assist others to this place when we understand how they are wired. The result is applied action personally, interpersonally, and professionally. With acquired and applied knowledge, we can actualize fuller potential. We can accept our individuality and see the individuality in others. A relaxed compassion arrives, judgment is halted, and oneness emerges.

BRIDGE and NAET Together

How to BRIDGE from Hidden to Healed: In a session, I clinically test the presenting symptoms to see if they are physical, chemical, and/or emotional. BRIDGE is utilized when emotion presents. NAET is utilized with chemical and physical presentation.

As we walk through life, our sensory system responds to our environment. There is an innate healing mechanism inside each of us attempting to "finish the symptom" and restore wholeness and harmony. When we experience a symptom, it is a historical vibration signaling, "I have felt this before." It is not new but an activated experience. The first response on the organism occurs electrodynamically. Therefore, healing must occur on this level of the being.

The meridian system in Traditional Chinese Medicine provides the framework, location, and pathways to find the hidden vibrations and bring them into healing and flow. Often restoration can be instantaneous. Other times there are layers to integrate vibrationally before symptoms resolve. Susceptibility is determined by many factors, such as genetic lineage, miasms, environment, lifestyle, and more. The magic happens as you discover that your root vibrations are unique and specific to you. You then move your symptom from "hidden to healed." It is worth discovering hidden (unconscious) root causes that can affect you daily. How can you thrive if you don't even know what is holding you back?

BRIDGE example: Many people have come to me with a long list of foods they must avoid as allergies and sensitivities are limiting their life. Countless times, a gluten or dairy sensitivity would present, and the roots originated in early infancy. In these cases, the emotional stories needed healing from a tender age when they had no conscious recall. As the mental/emotional level was integrated, the sensitivities no longer signalled.

NAET example: A man presented with a three-year headache. He tried a plethora of techniques to achieve relief. When I directly tested him, the energetic vibration showed that his meridian system was not in harmony with spices. It was affecting his Gallbladder pathway above his ear. As the vibration integrated through the meridian system with NAET, he achieved energetic balance, flow, and harmony.

BRIDGE example: Another client was experiencing overwhelming body shame and self-judgment and could simply not self soothe to fill the void. When we looked at the emotional root, it showed up as her experience in the womb. Her mother was self-critical of her body and was also smoking cigarettes. My client internalized the shame, discomfort, and addictive impulses from the in-utero experience. She felt like the womb was too small to be in wanted to kick her way out, and felt the rush of emotions that her tiny body could simply not understand, much less integrate. Within a few short minutes, she cleared layers of emotion and felt free, light, and amazing. The best news is that her impulses to overeat were understood, met, and cleared in a way that her conscious mind never would have figured out. Now she feels relaxed, peaceful, and in a state of complete trust.

The Magic of Rising from Our Depth

The magic of the rise is that our innate being is always seeking completion. When I began my practice more than fifteen years ago, the work seemed arduous and never-ending. It took longer for the vibrations of pain and separation to rise to the surface. There are moments of pain rooted in our past lives, soul amnesia, genetic lineage, our childhood, and our present lives. Defense mechanisms such as suppression, repression, denial, sublimation, and rationalization operate UNTIL we are safe and have the capacity to integrate overwhelming experiences. The elegance is experienced in the rise, integration, and ultimate healing.

When an innocent child is overwhelmed in an experience, many perceptions engage at once, igniting an oversupply of symptoms that an adult can dissolve. This is what trauma is and this is the elegance BRIDGE provides as critical mass is achieved and agony ends. All that you ever have been and will be resides and rises from hidden to healed in this now moment. What an opportunity to come to full life NOW!

You are more magnificent than you can possibly imagine; beautiful, pure, innocent, dynamic, and complete. Any experience of separation is simply an invitation home to the wholeness of your true nature, your Highest Self, your Divinity.

I invite your spirit to rise! Seek wholeness and actualize your completion!

Wholism Health
Separate to Whole...Hidden to Healed!

Whitney Merritt
Natural Health Practitioner

Whitney holds a mantle as an adept who has artfully blended three ancient practices into a modern, proficient and profound healing experience. Impossibly hidden causes from the most unlikely sources are found, logically explained and integrated into completion. As a very conscious human being, Whitney shares her knowledge generously with The Chart, NAET and her signature method, BRIDGE. Whitney delights in every client's freedom and true expansion.

whitney@thechart.ca

What 'Good to Greatness' Means to Me!
I believe in wholeness! Greatness arrived for me as I found individual signature within the collective ONE. Ancient methods blended into a path of healing for myself and othe I am thrilled to see the emergence of greatness, individually and collectively NOW. We are so much more than we can possibly imagine!

THE CHART
A process to discover how your innate personality operate increase mastery.

THE CHART shows you how your personality operates to:
- ○ Achieve mastery to live in alignment from your Higher Consciousness
- ○ End separation as you take your place within the Collective One
- ○ Understand THE CHART of loved ones, friends, colleagues, and more
- ○ Relax as peace and compassion replace confusion and judgements
- ○ Become your Highest Self and better relate to others with ease as you are
- ○ Tools which can end emotional and karmic pain fo ease, joy, purpose
- ○ Learn how to live OFF the chart: end duality and separation

Price: $225 for 90 Minute Session -
Discover your unique individual karmic signature

Scan QR code to book

www.thechart.ca

Internal Liberation: The RESET Collective

Christine Monaghan

The gap is where it's at! The gap is the empty space between your current circumstances and the future, next-best version of you, living new desires, visions, and goals. Liberation of circumstances and ways of being that no longer serve you closes this gap.

Why do so many choose not to close the gap or even take one step into the gap? *How* is why!

How stops most before they even get enthused about—never mind take action for—a future version of greatness! Why? Because it is easier to cancel oneself than risk the uncertainty of stumbling, or worse yet, failure. But is it really easier to cancel oneself versus be canceled per se? No. It creates suffering, regret, and doubt in so many ways, ultimately limiting the expansion of untapped potential, ease, and the joy of claiming "Wow, I did it—I really conquered *that*."

Many of our *hows* surface when forming goals because our limiting beliefs are attempting to keep us safe with the status quo, contained and comfortable. This is where the power of RESET practices can assist us to get comfortable being uncomfortable in incremental steps. If we can get emotionally attached to our desire (vision/goals), it greatly helps us to navigate through the muckiness of growth.

- Get clear on what and why of your desire first; imagine a future you, living greatness.

- Be OK not comprehending or knowing all the *hows* today; engage in the emotion of it first.
- Commit to daily due diligence to explore your desire or something even better.
- Train your mind to observe negative internal chatter and challenging external circumstances as a sign you're growing forward.
- See uncomfortableness as the sign you are progressing (change the story).
- Adopt a "source solutions" mindset to all perceived negatives that arise.

This is the *how.*

RESET practices are about sourcing solutions in the moment of awareness of fear, doubt, resistance, and all low-level vibes. These practices are about a "1 percent better moment-to-moment choice" toward what you do want and how you do want to feel and live. The RESET Collective (a group of like-minded business owners) thrives on:

- The power of proven RESET mindset and accountability tools and practices
- *Slow Down to Move Ahead* principles for innovation to do less way better
- A commitment for a referral-revenue-based business model

So, when is a RESET needed? In the moment of awareness of feeling less than focused, lacking productivity, weary and overwhelmed, apathetic, frustrated, stuck in the muck. Over time, you can reprogram your cellular makeup toward installing practices with repetition to spend less and less time in the lower-vibe moments, days, and weeks.

If not now, when?

If not you, who?

When I created the RESET Collective (six years ago), I had a vision for individual and collective greatness with and for business owners. If I had focused on all the *hows* and negative *what ifs* to get it up and running, I would never have embarked upon it. Every year it evolves into new levels of greatness from individual and collective collaborative contribution. I have immense pride and zero regrets for those I get to connect with, learn from, be inspired by, and collaborate with each day.

Did I know it would succeed starting out? No. Was I mutually excited and anxious about *how* it would work—or *if*? Yes. Was I 100 percent focused on the desired vision to the degree that I was willing to navigate stumbles and hurdles to grow toward the ideal? Yes. All things being equal, I trusted that the *hows* would present themselves if I focused on fulfilling my commitments to the members and sponsors to experience new levels of greatness. I like to say it has taken on a life of its own. This stems from individual and collective input, a willingness to make requested changes, energy, feedback, and love of those involved—an expansion of greatness with and for all. It continues to evolve.

Many say to me, "You are so focused, disciplined, and organized—I wish I could be that way." Well, yes, I am . . . NOW! I made a commitment to become this individual, knowing it would serve me and others to keep attaining that which I desire. Where did my discipline come from? A core principle is that we don't navigate all the highs, joys, wins, lows, sorrows, and griefs just because. We are here on Planet earth for a mysterious amount of time. We get the privilege of contributing to evolution while we're here. What a gift that is! What an honor! This drives my discipline and my why every single day.

With my coaching hat on to champion your greatness, liberation, and freedom, consider these questions:

- Where are you most often in terms of living your desired freedom experience?
- Do you need to sit your tush down and determine this?
- Is freedom part of your identity that leads to how your day unfolds? If not, why?
- Are you leading to not lose or leading for liberation to win and experience greatness?

- Do you allow uncomfortableness to drive the bus containing greatness that awaits you?
- What does mindset liberation mean to you?
- What is your relationship with yourself between your ears?
- Are you content to just be with yourself for hours on end? If not, why?
- Where do you need to say, "enough is enough," to make changes despite uncomfortableness?
- What will liberation from current circumstances mean for your expansion?

It is not easy facing and changing one's inner world to witness external greatness. It requires hard work in the form of repetitive, daily practices to grow into the next best version of you. Are you worth that work? Are you comfortable with an identity of struggle, chaos, or one of expansion, liberation, and freedom—every single day? Our results always show us where we are at. Managing our internal energy is a lifelong undertaking. To be relentless in this quest for liberation from limiting beliefs and circumstances is *how* greatness takes form.

Christine Monaghan
RESET for good to greatness results

Christine Monaghan
Owner

Christine is considered the 'go-to' RESET coach and trainer to close the gap between ones' current circumstances and those not yet realized. Her consulting company has impacted 1000's of solo-business owners and corporate teams in; referral-revenue-generation; reverse-engineering goal achievement; slowing down to move ahead mindset principles. Her 3C's of communication influence everything clients implement. Six years ago Christine created The RESET Collective - an online business owners training, mastermind, collaboration network. Recently, she launched SoloBiz RESET School - a hybrid of self-directed and live integration training. She has authored numerous books.

choiceswithchris@gmail.com

CHRISTINE MONAGHAN

www.christinemonaghan.com

What 'Good to Greatness' Means to Me!

We all want freedom for our lives. Experiencing freedom requires liberation of worn-out beliefs and life circumstances, expansion of ones' inherent greatness. How? Getting clear between a good life and one of greatness; 100% focussed action on that greatness; daily commitments, conversations, choices. Greatness is 1% better today than yesterday.

SoloBiz RESET Academy

What if you could access self-directed, methodical, easy to implement business principles and RESET practices to get from where you are to where you desire in your solo-biz? *What if* this included live integration training to establish results and source solutions along the way? You can!

- Self-directed programs, courses, e-books and templates
- Live integration calls; solutions for results
- Connect, collaborate with other SoloBiz owners
- Reasonably priced to elevate greatness, daily
- 24/7 access to all content, call recordings

7-Day SoloBiz RESET Challenge
Scan QR code to access!

You Are Worth the Journey!

Celeste Pennington

We are all capable of becoming our most authentic selves, and to do this, we must be brave enough to try something we have never done before. To say yes even when we are scared. My journey to becoming my greatest self started with a decision to join a MLM in 2016. I thought I was just saying yes to quality skincare, but what that yes represented in my life turned out to be the trajectory of so much more than my imagination was capable of even knowing at the time.

To be someone so bold that I now say yes constantly to things that scare me, to now being a multi-passionate entrepreneur with so many projects and ideas there isn't enough time in the day to do it all. Let's call the last six years "the road to Celeste," or "the journey to self—a road of liberation, mindset shifts, and self-compassion. When you say yes to an MLM opportunity, especially when you have never sold anything in your life, it will require you to grow. You have no choice. To learn about a product and share it with others takes guts, while you gain experience and confidence.

In the beginning, it was fun doing what people call a side hustle just to bring in a little extra income each month. However, things started changing in my husband's career. His job was causing him so much stress that he started having panic attacks before leaving every morning for his job in Toronto. We valued his mental health and wanted him to be a present father, and we knew he needed to leave that job and come home. So, we made a decision that I would start being serious with my side business, which meant I needed to level up my confidence. At the time that confidence was stuck in terrible self-worth paradigms. I knew

I needed some guidance, so I said yes to a mindset course that taught Bob Proctor methods, and this completely changed my life. I learned the framework for everything that was to come in my life.

One of the most important things I learned was that our mind is separate from our brain. Our thoughts become things, and our imagination is one of the most powerful tools we have. My side hustle did turn into a business, and my husband was able to quit his job and focus on his well-being.

A short time later, I came up with the idea of Earth Animals: kid's trading cards for younger kids. Within a year I had the product delivered to my door to be shared with the world. Again, thoughts become things— this is how creation works. Every time we learn more of who we are and what we are truly capable of, it requires new versions of ourselves.

Now, I was starting to get to know myself as an entrepreneur, not just as the title of my day job. I had to dig deep within again and learn how to run a business from scratch. I had to make the hard calls and decide how much of my own finances I was willing to put into my venture. This was also the time my husband and I decided it was time to head back to British Columbia and make it home. We loved raising our kids in Ontario, but they were starting to turn into indoor kids and needed the abundance of nature that BC has to offer. Using all the gifts I had learned about mindset, I manifested a job with higher pay located where we wanted to live, and everything came to us effortlessly within the year.

The universe really does look out for you, and everything that is meant for you will come easily. Visualize, hold the emotion, and trust.

Being surrounded in nature back in BC was nurturing. I continued to share Earth Animals with kids and businesses, continued to learn how to run a business with the support and knowledge that came from various master classes, and continued to kill it at my new day job.

The next turn in the road of my growth was not one of my choosing— but it's one that I will forever be grateful for. I had an adverse reaction to a shot, which opened my eyes to the world around me. This experience left me grieving a world and a life that didn't exist as I had known it. The pain is one of the rawest I had ever experienced. I had to dig deep to find the line I was not willing to cross, which left me on the outskirts because I was now not willing to continue with the façade.

When you go through this process, which we call an awakening, the only answer is your own truth. You have to stand in that truth even when others don't understand and challenge you. But every time this happens, you choose yourself. I learned to love myself despite others' approval. I no longer needed others' approval to be myself.

This was the beginning of the next version of myself, where I now learned about my spiritual gifts. I was forced to clear through old paradigms and old versions of myself, letting go of my ego and unconscious beliefs. I feel like I was able to see the true reality of the current world, and I consumed a lot of information quickly and because I was already aware of how to listen to my gut, I was able to sort through information objectively. I knew when to stop looking at information if it caused me to feel low and depressed. This was also my introduction to spiritual awareness and really tuning into the energy of things. With more learning on who we truly are as humans, which required unlearning so much, questioning everything, and then learning to trust my intuition to guide me. With months of this inner work, my fear went away—and when the fear leaves you, liberation starts and is so powerful. You come to realize that no one can hurt you and that you are already free.

Now starts the most powerful part of my story because by this point, I had released so much programming—all the stories I had told myself, all the labels others had placed on me, and all the limits society and myself had placed on me. Now it was time to rise—to connect with my higher self and know why I was now on earth at this time. I learned to look at all sides, discern at all levels, and even then, stay somewhat skeptical. My spiritual awareness really started to feel like the only truth. As I started seeing the world through my heart's lead lens, I became open to receiving information that my old self would have laughed at or ignored. Sometimes the words coming out of my mouth even make me laugh because they can sound so crazy to our current world.

We live on a planet within a galaxy, and everything is energy, frequency, and vibration. The physical body is only one component of our true self; we cannot see the mental, emotional, and spiritual aspects because they are thoughts, feelings, and heart, but they are real and impact our daily energy. We have 50 trillion cells in our bodies vibrating at all times. All organisms communicate with vibrations, which can alter our health and biology. Everything is energy, and frequency is the language of energy. The higher vibration we are, the healthier we are. Lower vibration makes us susceptible to poor health and disease.

Every cell, tissue, organ, emotion, thought pattern all has a frequency. Fear and love are also vibrations that sit on their own frequencies, and knowing how this earth works and understanding that we are all vibrating beings allows us to empower ourselves even further. We can use tools to keep ourselves in high vibration and thus not become susceptible to poor health and negative influences.

My "good to great" happened in layers and is continuing to evolve. It's our life journey to always be looking for ways to grow, and now that I understand frequency and vibration, I have been able to truly manifest whatever I want. I also manifested a tool that helps with my well-being on a daily basis, and because it is designed to play in the quantum field, the possibilities are endless. I am now tapping into quantum health and wealth with flow and ease as I share my calling on this earth, which is to help elevate the frequency of this planet. It happens one person at a time, each one elevating themselves. As we do this, we rise above the fear; we are free. We are sovereign beings who share our gifts with the world—a world that one day soon will be led with heart, integrity, and peace.

HEALY

What 'Good to Greatness' Means to Me!

First, you have to make a decision that you're ready to explore what can be possible for yourself in this lifetime. Second, some form of awareness that you are not where you want to be. Then you get brave by taking a chance on something you have never done before. YIKES and WOW! You have to be willing to explore parts of yourself that have been hidden. And, when it gets hard, you have to come back to your why, celebrate how far you have come and keep the vibration moving forward and keep going. Choosing yourself every time.

Celeste Pennington
Frequency Leader

Celeste is a multi-passionate entrepreneur. Recently she stepped into co-leading the Canadian Healy business division, to raise the vibration of this planet. Through her awakened journey, she is now creating the new! The HEALY device supports alignment of one's frequency for creation, abundance and health. Embarking on a new age of medicine is exciting to play a part in. Celeste is a mother to two boys and happily married to a man that is also on a soul path.

celestepennington@outlook.com
519-495-5487

HEALY DEVICE + COMMUNITY BENEFITS:

- Energetic alignment with the hottest, most sophisticated bio-hacking device to date
- Allow your entire being to bridge science and spirituality
- Reprogram and heal on a cellular level with:
  - Micro-frequency application
  - Healy enters cells, sends cellular frequency healing
- Address pain management - organs, tissues, mental health, spirit
- Be a customer or explore the business opportunity - unique and rare
- Be an early adopter of new era world energy, frequency and vibration solutions

What in your life do you want to improve? Ready to elevate your health and well-being and fly into the quantum and build generational wealth?

Curious to see how Healy can support you on this journey called life? Let's chat!

f ⓘ

www.canada.healy.shop

Beyond the Book: Strategies for Taking Your Publishing Game from Good to Great

Karen Strauss

> Greatness is not a function of circumstance. Greatness, it turns out, is largely a matter of conscious choice and discipline.
>
> —Jim Collins, Good to Great

In today's fast-paced world, publishing a book has become one of the most effective ways to share your ideas with the world. Writing a book is not just about putting words on paper—it's a profound experience that can help you turn good ideas into great ones. At Hybrid Global Publishing, we understand the transformative power of writing, and we help authors harness it to create impactful books that make a difference.

Writing Is a Transformative Experience

Writing a book is a transformative experience that can help you grow and evolve both personally and professionally. As you write, you start to clarify your thoughts and ideas, and this process often leads to new insights and perspectives. Writing also forces you to confront your fears, doubts, and insecurities, and this can be a powerful catalyst for personal growth.

As someone with more than thirty-five years in the publishing industry and the owner of my own publishing company, I recognize the life-altering power of writing. I've seen it over and over again in the lives of the authors with whom I've had the privilege of working. I'm an author myself, and I've learned how important it is to work closely with someone who can help fully harness this power. At Hybrid Global Publishing, we provide a supportive and collaborative environment that encourages our authors to be open and vulnerable, explore their ideas fully, and push the boundaries of their creativity.

Take Johnny, for example. When his spouse died, Johnny's life changed irrevocably. He had to figure out how to make a living, parent his grieving children, and work through his own grief. He felt like he wasn't enough. But he gradually realized that no matter how we choose to grieve, it will be enough regardless of what others think. He developed resilience to help his children get through the grieving process, and he discovered that he was strong and capable.

After working through the grieving process, he decided he wanted to share his story with others to help them move forward. Throughout the writing process, there were many ups and downs as he lived his story over and over again. At times, what seemed like a good idea was turning into something like a nightmare. But he persevered and eventually emerged on the other side with a published book he was proud of.

Through writing his book, he found hope, and that motivated him to start a coaching business to help other people move through their most devastating moments in life.

Writing a Book Requires a Proven Process

Once you are clear about your core message and the audience you hope to reach with your book, the next order of business is creating an outline. This will serve as your roadmap, guiding you along the way and keeping your focus when you begin to drift away from your central message. Then it's time to create a first draft. It will probably be terrible! However, once you've got a bad first draft, there's something to work with to make it good, and then even great. That's when the most important members of your team come into the picture: your editors.

Editing is the same as quarreling with writers—same thing exactly.
—Harold Ross

This quote by Harold Ross, the founder and first editor-in-chief of *The New Yorker* magazine, highlights the importance of editing in the writing process. Just as a quarrel with a writer can lead to a better, more refined idea, the process of editing a book can help to refine and improve the work, resulting in a more polished and professional final product.

Editing is an essential part of the writing process, and it plays a central role in transforming good ideas into great ones. Editing involves not just correcting spelling and grammar mistakes but also refining your message, clarifying your voice, and strengthening your key points.

As a publishing veteran, I understand the importance of editing, and I know how critical it is to work closely with our authors to ensure that their books are polished, professional, and impactful. Our team of experienced editors work collaboratively with authors to refine their message, clarify their voice, and elevate the quality of their writing.

Taking a good book and turning it into a great book is a challenging but rewarding process. Here are some tips that can help you improve your writing and take your book from good to great:

- *Refine your writing style:* Great writing is often characterized by its clarity, precision, and artistry. Pay attention to your word choice, sentence structure, and overall writing style, and consider how you can refine and improve it. Read widely and study the writing of other authors to get inspiration and insights.
- *Focus on storytelling:* People remember stories that have impact. If you are writing nonfiction, tell a story that illustrates the points you are making. Memorable stories are often what make a book great. If you are writing fiction, take the time to develop your characters fully, giving them depth, complexity, and unique personalities. Make sure they are relatable and have clear motivations and consider how they interact with one another to create conflict and tension.

- *Create compelling content:* Make sure you have a well-developed plot if you are writing fiction. A great book needs a strong and engaging plot that keeps readers hooked from beginning to end. Make sure your story has a clear structure, with well-defined arcs for your main characters. Consider using unexpected twists and turns to keep readers on their toes.

- Nonfiction requires a really tight outline and flow from beginning to end. Remember why you are writing this book in the first place (your purpose) and always keep in mind the benefit to the reader.

- *Use vivid and evocative language:* Great writing is often characterized by its ability to create vivid, sensory images in the reader's mind. Use strong, specific nouns and verbs, and come up with descriptive adjectives and adverbs that paint a clear, compelling picture for your readers.

- *Revise, revise, revise:* Great writing is the result of careful revision and editing. Take the time to review your work critically, looking for areas for improvement. Consider enlisting the help of beta readers who are willing to provide feedback.

- *Take risks:* To make your book truly great, you may need to take risks and push the boundaries of your genre or subject matter. Be willing to experiment with new approaches, styles, and themes, and don't be afraid to challenge your readers' expectations.

Putting Your Message Out into the World

Once your book is written and edited, the next step is to put your book out into the world. This can be a daunting task for many authors, but it's a crucial step in turning a good book into a great one. Book marketing ensures that readers are aware of you as the author as well as your book.

It's important to work with someone who can help provide comprehensive marketing and promotional services. This typically involves developing a customized marketing plan that includes speaking engagements, radio and podcast interviews, video content, and other promotional strategies.

Becoming the Go-To Expert in Your Field

One of the goals of publishing a book is to establish yourself as a go-to expert in your field. By sharing your ideas and insights with the world, you can position yourself as a thought leader and a trusted authority in your area of expertise. You can then seek out speaking opportunities and other outlets that reach your target audience and increase your reach. The more visibility you and your book generate, the more opportunities you will find to share your message and grow your audience of raving fans.

If you have dreamed of writing a book, there's no better time than now to get started. Remember, writing a great book takes time, patience, and dedication. Keep working on your craft, seek feedback and support, and stay committed to creating the best possible work you can.

Collaborative Effort and Energy

Going from good to great as an author requires collaborative effort and energy. Writing is a solitary activity, but it doesn't have to be a lonely one. Don't try to go it alone! Connect with a team that can support your vision and maximize your efforts. Ultimately, going from good to greatness as an author requires not just hard work and dedication but also a willingness to collaborate, to take risks, and to embrace the transformative power of writing. Having your own book in print is a real achievement—one that can open doors for you, help you to grow personally, and expand your business in a multitude of ways.

We are what we do repeatedly. Excellence then is not an act but a habit.

—Aristotle

Hybrid Global Publishing
We Take the Fear Out of Publishing

Karen Strauss
Owner/Publisher

Karen has held various positions in the Publishing industry for over 35 years. She has worked with celebrities such as President Jimmy Carter, Jimmy Stewart, Martha Stewart, George F. Will and Og Mandino. In 2010 Karen founded Hybrid Global Publishing, a firm that works with Entrepreneurs, Speakers, and coaches to help them write, publish, distribute, and promote their books in order to generate unlimited leads, get on more speaking stages, and grow their business by attracting more clients.

Karen has helped over 500 business owners become successful published authors and has helped 400 authors reach #1 bestselling status.

kbstrauss@gmail.com
646-232-9647

What 'Good to Greatness' Means to Me!

To move from good to greatness requires the consistency of servicing your clients well. Its about making the customer journey easy and collaborative as possible. We are always tweaking our publishing procedures, our offerings, and our way of communicati with our clients throughout the publishing process.

The Big Leap Retreat

The vast majority of aspiring authors can't get their book done, having tried solo for years only to let the dream go. What if your ideas are solid? Join the Virtual Big Leap Retreat; we will help you MUCH closer to delivering your important message to the world; ¶ most efficient and successful way possible.

- Unleash and get clarity to draw out your Big Idea; creative floodgates opened!
- Karen's signature 4-step formula; map out a bestselling book a weekend
- Create your 2-minute pitch; present to an A-List panel of movers and shakers at the retreat
- Work with experienced editors and publishers to map out yo book vision
- Complete the retreat with clarity, confidence, and direction; get your book across the finish line

Price: $197 USD

Scan the QR code to
register for our Retreat!

in f 📷

www.hybridglobalpublishing.com

Olympic Liberation Mindset

Krista Temple

Most people don't make the journey from good to greatness because of one fairly simple reason: They don't stick it out.

You cannot fail unless you give up!

It's not to say this simple fact makes it "easy." There is truly nothing harder than sticking it out. It's not easy to submit to the unknown, build new habits, and keep your nose to the grindstone, especially when you aren't seeing the results you want for your future in the shortterm. I believe if you have love for what you do, a strong driving force, and, finally, belief that you can accomplish what you desire, it will help you to endure the pressure of time.

I first sat in a boat during the summer of 2001. I immediately fell in love with the sport of rowing. I could see the dream of excelling in rowing early on. In Canada, you row at high school and or university, and from there, you have other racing opportunities at the provincial and national level. The national-level athletes compete for a spot on the Olympic teams. I looked up fitness scores of the national-team women and set my sights on being one of the best. I had finally found my sport.

I came from a very athletic household. My father was in constant pursuit of excellence on his mountain and road bikes, and at sixty-eight years old, you can still find him on the trails in Port Moody, BC. When I met rowing in 2001, I felt instantly connected . . . aligned. It became my main focus. To make the National team, to race on the World Championship stage, and finally make it to the Olympic Games. Representing out great country alongside some phenomenal women on the Olympic stage and winning a medal was such an honor!

My wish for you is to find that thing in life that lights you up, and when you find it, never let it go.

Mindset

On April 13, 2022, I was diagnosed with breast cancer. Facing cancer changes the whole life game quickly. Suddenly I found myself competing in a mental Olympics.

Mindset has been first and foremost my biggest ally and superpower. My list of the top ways I have kept my mind strong in the face of challenges and in the pursuit of excellence include:

1. **Be solution-oriented and stay in action.** Always stay open to solutions. There is always a way to stay in action of some sort. Choice is a way to navigate and gives a sense of control. When everything feels out of your control, what can you do? There is always something.

   The best practice is to focus on action and moving forward versus stalling or dwelling on what is behind you. You can only focus backward with respect to evaluating and making choices for the future. Take what you can from the past and set your sights ahead.

   In my rowing days, we made a point of controlling the controllables. There are so many variables in sport, in cancer, in business, and in life. We used the 1 percent strategy for performance. These were all the seemingly small additions we made to training and performance. Have confidence that all the little ways you are working toward your best performance or success will add up to much more than 1 percent. Pilates, diet additions and restrictions, scientific input on boat rigging, beet juice shots before races, the visualization—all of these little initiatives took us from good to great. Never underestimate the ability of many small contributions to your success over time.

2. **Take responsibility for your mindset.** You, and only you, are responsible for your thoughts and how you perceive your circumstances. You can adjust to see anything and everything however you choose. Having a positive mindset is a choice. There is a fighting spirit to mindset. We can waste our time fighting and

battling ourselves mentally, and or we can harness our power for action. I have been told countless times that I have been brave during my cancer journey. But what choice did I have? My choice was to believe it would all be OK, and I would not go down without a fight. There really is no other way. I am here to fight this battle.

3. **Course-correct when necessary.** Picking yourself up by the bootstraps and figuring out your new way takes discipline and self-awareness. I had a low moment after I was through chemotherapy and got the results post-surgery. What was left behind was frustratingly close to what was measured to be there to start with. They also found a suspect deposit, which brought my surgical oncologist's original decision to get a lumpectomy versus a mastectomy into question. I then chose to have a second surgery to remove all breast tissue.

    This was a moment. I felt discouraged and angry, to say the least. I had spent thousands of dollars on naturopathic treatment as well as faced chemotherapy and all that goes with it, and still the cancer didn't budge.

    It was my naturopath that helped me reframe and move forward. We realigned and made a plan for where our attention was best spent, and that was on moving forward and not staying in the past. There is so much unknown when it comes to cancer, so much we will never know. For me, it's been a life lesson on a grand scale.

    It is so important to move through failure—to learn from your successes and your mistakes and maintain a positive attitude.

4. **Have the courage to set ambitious goals.** Napoleon Hill said it best: "Whatever the mind of man can conceive and believe, it can achieve." Lofty goals are where the good stuff happens. Learn to see the big vision and have confidence in what is possible in this world. There is so much focus on short-term goals, but what about the big vision? The six-figure income, the million-dollar business idea, the Olympics!

    This lofty goal-setting part of me went dormant after the Olympics. I think I was overwhelmed with the idea that I had to top it. Rowing was an opportunity that came along at the right place and at the right time, and I seized it. After I retired, I believed that another opportunity would present itself to me. I just didn't know when, and I didn't necessarily realize how much this future opportunity would be impacted by my mindset and openness to receive the opportunities the universe shared with me.

I retired from rowing in 2013, and I started my family in 2016. I have two beautiful children and an amazing and dedicated husband. I have so much to be grateful for. I always say that people deserve Olympic medals for these life successes. Real life is hard, folks!

It is now 2023, and I am seizing a new goal and dream. I now aspire to build a financial fortress for my family. This is my new life's ambition, my new reason to get up and go. As a stay-at-home mother, I haven't recently had much time to focus on my own personal achievements, but now is a new time to be seized. We all have different seasons in life, and it's OK not to have everything you desire on an exact timeline. The goal is to stay inspired by your dreams and never lose that ambition.

A Love Letter

What advice would I give to someone good who wants to be great? Always maintain a sense of hope and peace in the journey of life. Worrying is just negative goal-setting. You will attract more and become more like whatever it is you think about most, so make it good! Free yourself from the pressure of curating an end result. We aren't able to see into the future, so control what you can and always go after what makes you happy.

At the end of the day, it's just you and yourself. Develop and foster a strong belief in your abilities because this will carry you through. Do this by saying yes to opportunities that stand out and align with all that you are. Visualize your success and embody who you want to be and what you want in your life. Find a way to make those things happen. Have the courage to take calculated risks and make the most of every opportunity that comes your way. The love you have for what you do is what will fuel you to persevere when it gets tough. If you truly want something, you will find a way.

Finally, know that in the hard times you are practicing resilience that will serve you in your future battles. Don't try to dodge the big feelings and the hard times because they are uncomfortable. In fact, get super comfortable with being uncomfortable because that will also serve you. You are strong beyond measure, and when you put your mind to something, you cannot fail!

Krista Temple
Enagic Distributor

The pillars of Krista's work and life are health, clean living, mindset and family. Krista is a daughter, sister, wife, and mother first and foremost. She is also a 2x Olympian, silver medalist, author and as of 2022 she is a breast cancer warrior.

kristaleightemple@gmail.com
(778) 838-5904

What 'Good to Greatness' Means to Me

Relentlessly pursuing what you want in life takes a seemingly small and good vision to unbelievable heights of greatness. A fearless approach involves courage and calculated risks; never making excuses; seeing failures and setbacks as learning; 100% focus on moving forward. It's about giving back to the world; a picture world-class mentality for your life vision; doing what you love with pride; and commitment to an unbreakable spirit. Greatness is yours!

Be H20 Healthy; Create Freedom Income

Water is literally ones way to health or lack thereof. What if you could access water health on a new level to fuel your optimum health and have the option to establish generational wealth? This system does both.

- Japan based, international distributor; delivering thousands of Kangen Water machines globally
- Medical grade water ionizers; transform tap water into pure, healthy, electronically reduced and hydrogen-rich drinking water
- Anespa Dx Home Spa System transforms your bathroom into a natural hot spring
- Access to a high caliber online community to assist in building your business
- Self-paced training plus peer guidance 24/7
- Combine high-ticket sales with automation for income stream and time freedom

View 30-minute web class to learn more
Scan QR code to view!

KRISTA TEMPLE
Independent Distributor at Enagic
WWW.KRISTATEMPLE.COM

f ⓘ

www.kristatemple.com

Trust Yourself

Jo-Anne Weiler

"Who hasn't been challenged in life?" I say to myself as I'm sitting in the hallway of Richmond Hospital, waiting to go in for surgery to have thirty-five-year-old breast implants taken out. Am I nervous? Yes, of course, I am. I'm wondering to myself how I ever said yes to putting a foreign object under my pectoral muscles so close to my heart.

I'm considering what the chances are that the breast tissue has connected somehow to my heart. And if I'd just loved my body, after having produced two babies and nursed for almost four years total, I wouldn't be sitting here fighting off my anxiety.

I'm a registered clinical counselor and marriage and family therapist, so I began to coach myself. "Breathe, Jo-Anne . . . try your tapping," I said to myself. All my tools seemed in the moment to evade me, so I headed to the washroom down the hall to do the exercise I know works the best—i.e., shaking my whole body for a minute and then feeling the oxytocin rush in to calm me down.

I walked back, and then heard my name called. It was time.

I smiled when the prep nurse said, "You are such a centered person . . . so calm." I felt so grateful for her, for the hospital, and for my surgeon who arrived shortly after.

And here I am now, two months later, all myself again—implant-free and so thankful for the plastic surgeon who reconstructed my natural breasts that suffered the poor decisions I made in my late twenties.

Trust Your Gut

What a journey! I had wanted my "saline" implants to be taken out ten years earlier but was turned down by the original surgeon who said, "There is no medical reason to have these out."

Still, my gut told me they should be removed.

I went back to him three times over those ten years and was sent away each time with the same advice. It wasn't until late this past summer when, exasperated, I finally asked my GP, "Why can't I have these implants out?" And he said, "Of course, you can. Let's get an MRI as a first step."

The MRI confirmed that my implants were partially silicone, not 100 percent saline as I had been led to believe. The rest is history. I went to another plastic surgeon on the other side of the city, a woman who totally understood what I was going through. She said, "Let's get these out."

What lessons did I learn from this long breast implant tug-of-war with my doctors? There are times we need to advocate for ourselves and trust our gut to push through roadblocks. I believe there is a gift we all have—to know in our bodies what decisions are best. We can tune in and trust our intuition. This internal message board can be a massive resource in how we conduct our lives.

As I've reflected on my life, I can recall numerous times when I've just known the right course of action because of a compelling infusion of intuition. I didn't have that clear sense of trusting my gut in my twenties. If I had, I likely wouldn't have got the implants in the first place! Maybe relying on our intuition is a cultivated source of wisdom. Certainly, trusting oneself is a learned process.

Life Is Full of Magic

Last year, I entered a tennis tournament at our club and was assigned a partner. It's a fun social tournament in which people bet on you (in a Calcutta format) if they think you are a strong team to win. I was matched with another gal who (like me) was a good but not great player.

There we stood at the front of the room with forty other tennis players, many of whom were superstars paired with beginners.

The room was silent when it was our team's turn to be wagered on. We stood there, feeling a little humiliated when no one bet on us. I smiled as I broke the silence to say, "I'm going to bet on US!" With that, the room roared with laughter. And as we left the pretournament party, I said to my partner, "No worries . . . she who has the most fun wins. We've got this."

Miracle of miracles, the next day we filled the court with giggles and good shots and came away with the trophy. I'll never forget my partner jumping in the air with glee and saying, "This is the most fun I've had all year!" I'm not sure what fueled our success that day, but what I know for sure is that when the whole-body brain is calm, focus goes up and performance rises. It still makes me smile thinking of that tournament.

Life is full of magic when we trust ourselves. Sometimes looking ahead at the prize just puts you in the zone.

Another small miracle happened during a multigenerational "girls' trip" to New Zealand with my mom and my then-ten-year-old daughter. We took a boat trip along the coastline up north to a small town called Russell. And I said yes to participating in a dive into a deep-sea cave.

I swam toward a long passage that flowed into a relatively small rock opening. As the passage narrowed, we were instructed to file in one by one. Swimming deeper into this cavern, I started to sense the walls closing in and my heart rate going up. We were further told that as the tides were high, we would need to hold our breath and kick as hard as possible to move through the narrow underwater space of a few hundred feet to reach the deep-sea cave inside.

Talk about having faith! But there I was, moving along in single file. There was no turning back at this point. The passageway, as promised, narrowed to something slightly wider than the width of my body. Half the participants were behind me, and half were in front of me. I'm a good swimmer, but if I swam too fast underwater, I'd swim into the person ahead of me. . . . The bottom line was that I had to trust the people in front of me to keep on swimming. And several people behind me were counting on me to do the same! If I panicked and altered my pace, others in the group might do the same, and who knows what would happen then?

I just clicked myself into that state of trust in the Universe—full commitment! Determined, I held my breath, swam through the cool water, and kicked as hard as a I could, all while fighting off the urge to give in to a full-blown panic attack. And I made it! We finally emerged from the long, narrow water tunnel. By trusting ourselves and our group to work in unison, we were able to transit the subterranean passage to its destination where we stood in awe with one another in a beautiful, sparkly quartz rock cave. We all just beamed as we enjoyed this shared embodied delight from one of nature's hidden miracles.

As I looked up, there was a slight opening in the rocks above and a bright shaft of sunlight; it felt like divine confirmation, as though the Universe was saying, "Well done."

Building Blocks to Trust

What are the building blocks to achieving a sense of deep trust? How do we hold on to an expectation that we have what it takes, that we can do IT? It starts by getting better at choosing what IT is that we want.

It helps to have had a secure start in life. What were you doing at eighteen months? A well-researched theory of psychosocial development put forth by Erik Erikson is that we learn to trust in the time between birth and eighteen months.

Most of us don't have memories of what we experienced earlier than age five or six. But if you have struggled with anxiety or decision-making, it's time to start to train your whole-body brain back to what you knew as an infant before any misinformation started messing with you.

You are amazing, complete, wonderful and a gift to our world. If you don't know that already, start paying attention to all the big and little things you do every day that prove you are a beautiful miracle. And when you reflect on those not-so-shiny moments, just remember how you learned to walk. You fell, you skinned your knees, and then you discovered better balance.

What confusing messages confound our own amazing life experiments? We should all be rocking joy every step of our adult lives.

Attachment theory suggests that as, infants, when we go through this early stage of experiencing trust versus mistrust, how we emerge from this journey is a foundation of how well we thrive later in life. In short, in the early stages of life, if our needs are met by a nurturing caregiver, we learn to trust that we are safe and our needs matter to others.

The whole-body brain gym is to get back to the YOU that you were at birth. Trust that you are a perfectly imperfect human. You deserve. You are good. In fact, you are GREAT! The truth is that the more you know that, the better all your relationships will be because that knowing gives you a foundation to be present and open, even in stressful times.

Healthy relationships lead us all to live longer lives. The more bonded we are, the more stability and love we experience in all parts of our life. The more we are loved, the more we expect to be loved, and the less at risk we feel when confusion or chaos happens.

In times of stress, like during our global pandemic, those with a secure attachment style can act like a team, even feel like part of the global team. The more you trust yourself and feel secure in our world, the less chaotic your life will feel. These are global truths and have been proven out in scientific research.

It's Your Time

This is your life. It's time to engage because life is just not going to come to you. We are all living our own unique lives, with our own unique wisdom, our own unique style of what our best life looks like. What is your style? What are you passionate about? What is your truth? That all sounds so clichéd as I write this, but honestly, it's taken me a few decades to deeply understand all this, especially the importance of TRUST. Trust that every action and reaction is exactly on purpose for your highest good. There truly are no mistakes. I love this quote: "There is a crack in everything, it's how our light shines through." Let your cracks shine bright!

I followed my intuition back to health this past year. I bet on my tennis partner and me amidst a roomful of much more talented tennis players, and we won based on our trust in each other and our sense of joy for the game. I swam into a dark, deep, narrow tunnel with strangers and found a stunning, sparkly cave. Trust is built through all these moments. Trust in yourself and know that you are a magic maker.

Jo-Anne Weiler
Get Your Love Up!

Jo-Anne Weiler
Life / Relationship Coach
BA, MA (Psych), CPCC, RCC, RMFT, CAMFT, ICF

"A warrior for the heart," Jo-Anne helps individuals and couples re-discover their own vitality and inner strengths. Igniting the spark in her clients capacity to live fully with joy and flow.

Jo-Anne has worked in psychotherapy for over 20 years. She is also a Professional Life Coach, author, public speaker, and has been featured on CBC, CTV, and various radio broadcasts. Jo-Anne is known for her energy, creativity, and leadership which she brings to any group she works with.

What 'Good to Greatness' Means to Me!

I believe we all have greatness within us and a purpose unique to our souls. One of life's greatest challenges--to trust we have within us, everything we need to live fully. A greater force is at play when we let go, we join a higher global greater intention. I know there is a counterpoint in us all that is deeply good and a source of great potential... and when we feel connected to that greater good, we live with JOY and FLOW.

6-WEEKS TO YOUR BEST

Therapy | Coaching program

- Held weekly or bi-weekly
- Individual or couple focused
- Resource your strengths and activate positive change
- Build your communication toolbox & develop your team at work & home
- Develop your personal blueprint to Love with Full Wingspan

Price $1,710

Alternative Options (GST applicable)

- Individual | Couple's session(s): $190 per hour
- 'Lunch and Learn': $700 per session or $2000. Series of 4
- Retreat 1/2 day: $250 per person (min. 4)
- Retreat 1 day: $400 per person (min. 4)
- 'Your Joy Adventure' Retreat: tailored destination retreats
  5 ½ day sessions

Price $2,000 + Expenses

Your Time Is Now, Get Your Love Up.
Scan QR code to book!

in f 𝕏

www.joanneweiler.com

The Flight of an Entrepreneur

Christie Wengranowski

Building your business is a journey full of lessons that give you so much wisdom if you can be open to receiving it. Establishing and elevating is all about the growth of the person plus simple systems and practices based on the nature of the business. Almost two decades into owning my small business with a team of three, I've come to realize five principles that have created and elevated my game, and I truly believe these can work for every business owner.

My Journey

I was born to be an entrepreneur. I was not taught how to be one, however. If you asked me what I was at twenty-five years old, just starting out, my answer would have been, "I own a graphic and web design business," and that was about it.

Today, I will tell you I am an entrepreneur who helps companies refresh their brand identity to reflect how they have grown, speak to whom they serve, and clearly articulate why someone should hire them. My experience in brand development lends a hand to increasing profitability for my clients and gives them marketing tools to help them excel. The team that supports me has a wealth of knowledge and talent that goes into creating solutions that make a difference to each business we help.

Today, I am a leader, not a boss, and creating a healthy work environment is paramount to the success of my business. My team respects one another, puts in maximum effort, and genuinely loves what they do. As an entrepreneur, I am a creator, leader, and innovator. This is a massive shift in mindset from twenty-five-year-old me who just wanted to have a business and help people.

Let me be very honest: Entrepreneurship wasn't an easy start for me, not by a long shot. It was full of financial hardship, tax stress, a few crazy or mean clients, and flying by the seat of my pants. The first eight years, I had a business partner on whom I relied instead of taking more initiative to figure things out on my own. When she took time off to have her first child, it was a big wake-up call for me. I saw what I wasn't taking responsibility for and how that was hurting me and our company. When she had her second child, we decided it was time to part ways so she could focus on family and I could focus on my career (which I was finally ready to really do). No more relying on others—this was my chance to step up and grow.

The partnership wrapped up amicably, leaving our friendship strong and likely seeing us as pals well into old age. It was my time to change, and with that top of mind, I rebranded the company with a new name: Flying Horse Design Studio.

This name holds meaning for me not just because I am an equestrian, but more so because Pegasus is a horse that can fly. I saw this business change as an opportunity to spread my wings and fly upward into the next phase of life. That resonates each time I level up and grow. Therefore, the name will always be very fitting.

In 2012, I was flying solo as Flying Horse Design Studio, and my love for what I was doing, along with a lot of persistence, helped me move into what I had envisioned the company to be. It was the next level of my journey and the realization of my self-worth. To be clear, this was still only the start of my growth; there was so much more to learn, and it has been quite the ride.

Building my house of business started with experimentation, making mistakes, fixing them, taking on risks, and wondering if I would ever figure things out. The funny thing was that all along I was creating something so powerful that it would game-change my business. Despite not seeing it at first, I was consistently leveling up, kicking complacency out the door, getting very uncomfortable, and pushing through challenges. The level of discomfort was so great at times that I would sweat, feel light-headed, and want to puke. Uncomfortableness aside, this was a long-term renovation plan to ensure that everything stayed current and up to code, just like a physical house.

As I became aware of the power behind this consistent business renovation, it was clear that this was part of moving my brand from good to great. It was the revelation I wasn't expecting, and it gave me such clarity on how to amplify the design work my team provides, not only to up our game, but also our that of our clients.

Five Principles to Establish, Maintain, and Scale a Business

I've found the following five principals to be instrumental in establishing, maintaining, and scaling Flying Horse. My growth with each one has moved me forward to new levels I didn't think were possible, and I know any business owner can do this, too.

1. **Invest in Personal development.** Investing in my development as a person and as a leader was the most important step. Mindset is everything, and if you have a poor mindset, your choices, actions, and reactions can destroy a business quickly. Taking emotional intelligence training followed by leadership courses gave me valuable tools and allowed me to build an epic team. It also gave me tools to untangle uncomfortable situations in a way that left upset parties feeling calm and good about moving forward.

2. **Hire a Business coach.** Hiring a business coach to help me design processes, keep me accountable, and push me out of my comfort zone has been invaluable. My weekly calls help me identify blind spots, rein me in when I get off track, and serve as an outside resource for many valuable things. I don't always like what I hear, but the key has been to remain coachable and try things on to see how they unfold.

3. **Participate in a community.** Finding a tribe to belong to was something I resisted for the first ten years of my business. I didn't see the value, and the few experiences I'd had were disappointing. One thing I cannot stress enough is to find a group of like-minded people

whom you vibe with, and then show up and contribute. Combined wisdom is powerful for growth, and hearing others go through the same things you do makes being in business easier. Sometimes it takes testing out a few groups to find the right one, but when you find it, the people in this group will have your back as you will have theirs. They will happily refer you to others, and you can do the same.

4. **Build Strong marketing Materials.** Design and messaging matter in your marketing materials, no matter what you do. Sure, I have a team of designers—it's what we do—but every business needs good representation to sell their product or service. Invest in your brand identity; it's the visual communication tool that tells people they need what you have. I strive to use a consistent, clear brand look and feel on our website, social media, sales sheets, print items, contracts, and whatever else we send out to ensure our brand lands well with clients. Two or three times a year, I review what we're doing and refresh it, and once every three years, I do a bigger brand refresh and update the design to be relevant to the way we have grown.

5. **Have a recharge Station.** I have a passion outside of my business, and this gives me balance in my life. What I do in my business and career is very fulfilling, and it's something I love; however, it's important to prevent burnout and refuel. For me it's riding my horses, working around the farm, and enjoying being outside. Stepping away from my business allows me to do better in it. Don't work your life away! Enjoy it, live it, and you'll be better in business because of it.

In creating a business you love, there are so many elements that contribute to your success. The five principles I've shared have made a massive difference in my business and life, and they have done the same for many of my clients. The key is to show up, be accountable, and take responsibility for yourself and your business. Nobody else can do it for you. When you show up for yourself, the pride that comes with what you accomplish on the journey is immeasurable and worth every moment you invest.

Flying Horse Design Studio

Creating revenue generating design to help grow your business

Christie Wengranowski
President / CEO

Christie has a passion for transformation through the medium of graphic and web design. A love of art and entrepreneurial spirit led her to creating her business at 25. Christie's experience in brand development enables her to develop visual solutions to help businesses increase profitability and excitement around their brand.

christie@flyinghorsedesignstudio.com
778-298-1119

What 'Good to Greatness' Means to Me!

To me, it means innovating what and how I lead by; working smarter; providing superior 'wow' value to my clients from the moment we initially connect; feeling empowered alignment with crystal clear vision. This results into loving what I offer and why, resulting in client fulfillment.

Brand Refresh 2023 (My Signature Offer)

A methodically simple yet impactful approach to refine and refresh your brand message visuals to enhance your offerings.

Includes:
- Your logo design + business card look/feel upgrade
- Co-creation Promotion Sheet; your #1 marketing prospecting tool
- Five new graphic assets (icons/patterns/textures) for social media, web, and Canva
- Brand Style Guide (fonts/colours/logo usage)
- One social media banner image for; Facebook; IG, Linkedin
- Five social media image templates for brand consistent posting

Complementary 30-min. 'Refresh Brand' Check-Up
Value = $175

Scan QR code to book!

FLYING HORSE
DESIGN STUDIO

in f ⓘ

www.flyinghorsedesignstudio.com